Angel After

Shades of Grief, Guilt and God

Christi L. Leveille

Foreword by Keven Leveille

Copyright © 2020 Christi L. Leveille

All rights reserved. No part of this book may be used or reproduced by any means, graphic, electronic, or mechanical, including photocopying, recording, taping or by any information storage retrieval system without the written permission of the author except in the case of brief quotations embodied in critical articles and reviews.

This book is a work of non-fiction. Unless otherwise noted, the author and the publisher make no explicit guarantees as to the accuracy of the information contained in this book and in some cases, names and places have been altered to protect their privacy. *The views expressed in this work are solely those of the author.*

Because of the dynamic nature of the Internet, any web addresses or links contained in this book may have changed since publication and may no longer be valid.

Scripture taken from the New King James Version ®. Copyright © 1982 by Thomas Nelson. Used by permission. All rights reserved.

Scripture quotations taken from the New American Standard Bible ® (NASB), Copyright © 1960, 1962, 1963, 1968, 1971, 1972, 1973, 1975, 1977, 1995 by The Lockman Foundation. Used by permission. www.Lockman.org. All rights reserved.

Scripture quotations taken from the Holy Bible, New Living Translation, Copyright © 1996, 2004, 2015 by Tyndale House Foundation. Used by permission of Tyndale House Publishers, Inc., Carol Stream, Illinois 60188. All rights reserved.

Scripture taken from the King James Version of the Bible ©. All rights reserved.

Scripture quotations taken from the Holy Bible, New International Version ®, NIV®. Copyright © 1973, 1978, 1984, 2011 by Biblica, Inc. ™ Used by permission of Zondervan. All rights reserved. www.zondervan.com. The "NIV" and "New

International Version" are trademarks registered in the United States Patent and Trademark Office by Biblica, Inc.

ISBN: 9798696998626

Library of Congress Control Number: 2018675309

Printed in the United States of America

To anyone who has ever suffered a tragic blow to
your self-worth by the hands of trauma;

To anyone who has ever abandoned the beautiful for
a more intimate embrace of all that is ugly;

To myself;

If ever you drift into a place in which your identity
becomes cloudy and your value unrecognizable;

Remember God desires to restore you and remind
you of just how powerful and beautiful you truly are.

To my loving husband and partner in life, Keven
Leveille; You still are God's perfect expression of His
love towards me. *Ou se enspirasyon mwen.*

To my babies, Angel Taylor and Michael Angel,
you taught me so much about myself.
We will see you both again one day.

To everything there is a season,
A time for every purpose under heaven:

A time to be born,
And a time to die;
A time to plant,
And a time to pluck what is planted;
A time to kill,
And a time to heal;
A time to break down,
And a time to build up;
A time to weep,
And a time to laugh;
A time to mourn,
And a time to dance;

Ecclesiastes 3:1-4 (NKJV)

Contents

Foreword x
Introduction xvi
Angel Taylor 1
    Ugly 2
    Vibrant 4
    Giddy 6
    Mini 8
    Special 10
    A Time to Pray 12
    Dim 14
    Gray 16
    A Time to Weep 18
    Still 21
    A Time to Release 22
    Pink 24
    A Time to Cope 25
    Empty 27
    A Time to Mourn 29
Michael Angel 31
    Uncertain 32
    A Time to Believe 33
    Light 35

Low 36
A Time to Declare 38
Bright 39
Expectant 42
Little 43
A Time to Hear 46
Pain 49
Tested 52
A Time to Release 57
Blue 59
Numb 61
A Time to Move 62
Undone 63
A Time to Chill 66

After Angels **67**

Guilt 68
Night 69
A Time to Be 71
Red 74
Flawed 76
A Time to Travel 79
Green 81
Dark 83
A Time to Watch 86

> A Time to Rebuild 89
>
> *God Is* **91**
>
> > God Is My Comfort 92
> > God Is My Strength 98
> > God Is My Creator 101
> > A Time to Dance 105
>
> Acknowledgements **109**

# *Foreword*

by Keven Leveille

That day is unforgettable. Michael Angel in all of his one-pound of chocolate glory alive in the palm of my left hand. His ears tucked neatly under a blue and pink striped beanie. A thick smear of black brows framed each eye neatly. His nose small. His lips thin. His skin slightly translucent. His entire existence resting in the palm of my left hand. Head. Neck. Torso. Arms. Hands. Legs. Feet. Ten Fingers. Ten Toes. He was bone of my bones, flesh of my flesh and alive.

When the nurses led me to the back room, I could tell by the look on the doctor's face that something was wrong. Although this was our first live birth, it was not our first time experiencing trauma. Christi and I had become particularly familiar with the presence of dread. We knew sorrow and fear also. The doctor's eyes were possessed with all three. She appeared ready to give up on Michael but with much apprehension. She seemed to be waiting on my permission to release her to make her expert pronouncement. She was about an hour into a fight to keep Michael alive. After examining my face and not finding that release, no give in my expression, she continued with chest compressions.

1 – 2 – 3 - pause. 1 – 2 – 3 - pause. 1 – 2 – 3 - pause. With each pause, the doctor looked up at me. Searching my eyes. Examining my face. Perhaps looking for some indication that I was remotely aware of what she already knew. That Michael could not be saved. That it was time to let him go. With each compression I asked Michael to come back. To be strong. To "do it for your mom." I wasn't ready to give up.

As the compressions continued, eventually the doctor looked up at me and asked if I wanted to try. The answer was an emphatic yes. I could not give up. Perhaps God wanted to display His miracle working power and use me to perform it. I immediately began summoning every ounce of faith I had left in the depleted reservoirs of my spirit to burst forth and assemble in my right thumb. We needed a miracle and God was able to perform it.

They placed my son Michael in my left hand. He wedged in neatly. His bare delicate skin against my sweaty palm. With my right thumb, I began chest compressions as instructed. 1 – 2 – 3 – come on son. 1 – 2 – 3 – do it for your mom. 1 – 2 – 3 – come on son. 1 – 2 – 3 – live. The rhythm I remember vaguely. The intensity in which I prayed, I'll never forget. I was stirring up with faith, rebuking death, knowing God was able. Believing He would respond despite the doctor's disbelief. Michael's heart rate began spiking on the monitor. I felt encouraged. I knew we would be ok. Michael would make it. I continued with compressions. But whenever I stopped, Michael began to flatline. So, I started up again. When I stopped, he flatlined. I continued again. And again.

More nurses walked in to watch. Each of them displaying dread, sorrow or fear. The doctor appeared dejected. Still searching my face. Waiting for me to accept what was obvious to her while also being respectful of my desire to exhaust my faith. I begged God to do it for Christi. I desperately wanted my son to live also, but I knew Christi needed this miracle. She needed God's display of mercy. She needed our son to live. My heart broke at the thought of what this could do to her. The compressions continued.

About thirty minutes later, the door to the room swung open and two nurses rolled in a stretcher carrying my wife. Christi appeared relatively conscious but clearly still groggy from drugs and understandably still in pain from delivery. My mind began to drift. I wondered why they would allow her back here under the circumstances but instantly the answer came to me. I knew. They were letting her say goodbye. My heart dropped. I thought a prayer. God, if there was ever a perfect time to work a miracle, it is right now. Lord please do not allow me to have to search for the words to tell my wife, we lost another one. God, do this for Christi.

Without any additional details of what was going on with Michael, the doctor looked at Christi and said "We've been trying to resuscitate him. Should we keep trying?" I was a bit puzzled. I'm sure the doctor did not expect Christi to answer in the negative. Why not just let her know we were trying to save Michael? Was Christi wheeled in because I said keep going and the doctor wanted a second opinion? Or perhaps the doctor was simply allowing Christi to actively get involved with the resuscitation as well. Christi also answered with an emphatic yes. The compressions continued. Michael struggled to breathe.

Panic and faith began to well up in me. The room was so saturated with defeat and death that I chose to step into the hallway. I needed air. I had a limited window to wrestle with my faith, to provoke a miracle, and I couldn't be distracted. Whose report will you believe? *I'll believe the report of the Lord.* I thought of the statement made by one of the three Hebrew boys. *God, You are able to deliver us from our circumstances but even if You don't.* (Daniel 3:17-18, NKJV) WAIT - PAUSE. What if He does not come through. He can. But what if He does not. I began to pray but I also questioned my faith. Was it enough…enough to provoke the hand of God? Was I close enough to Him to sneak a word in? To get to His ear? I prayed anyway. I walked up and down that hallway and I prayed.

When the nurse called me back in the room and said there was nothing more they could do, we barely flinched. We were either displaying radical faith or simply too numb from shock to process the pronouncement. Christi and I took turns holding our son. They wrapped him in a multi-colored blanket and handed him to me. I caressed his forehead with my finger. Still believing God could do it. I examined the details of his face. Christi adjusted her hospital gown slightly and I handed Michael over. She held his face to her bare chest. Skin to skin. She stared at him for a moment. And I watched them both, completely unaware of the darkness awaiting that moment to end just to sneak in and envelope us. Nothing could have prepared us for what was next.

I have had the pleasure of traveling this journey with Christi. I've shared her joy and felt her pain. I've seen her heart shatter in countless pieces and I've been motivated by her sheer courage. I've witnessed her struggle to roll out of bed and I've watched the power of God restore her strength. I've been praying for the miracle power of God and I now see it displayed in my wife. For a season she was mute - muzzled by depression, but now she is declaring victory from the mountain top of freedom. Her once blinded eyes now see with keen perspective. Dead passions have been resurrected. Christi is my miracle. Often times we can exhaust ourselves in our efforts to obtain a thing that we don't have the strength to appreciate the abundant blessings and miracles all around us. God is still working miracles. Christi is my tangible reminder of how God favors me. She is my goodness and mercy. She is God's love personified. She is my miracle.

After Angel takes us on a journey through overwhelming joy at life, to traumatic pain at death, through depression and doubt and to the enlightenment that despite our misfortunes, God still is and we still are.

Introduction

Angel After started out as a series of journal entries—my attempt at therapeutic release from the aching emotions threatening to poison me from within. My journal became a necessary outlet from trauma experienced during a very dark chapter in my journey, losing my Angels. Nothing could have sufficiently prepared me for the rollercoaster of emotions that losing a child would force upon me. With the loss of my Angels, my concept of identity, the assurances of my self-worth and my conviction to live began to slowly deteriorate. I was no longer free to be happy and it became increasingly difficult to breathe. Initially, I wrote to release. Then ultimately, I wrote to survive as I began to sink deeply and rapidly into the hollows of depression.

Solomon says in Ecclesiastes Chapter Three, *"there is a time for weeping,"* and I wept. He says, *"there is a time for mourning,"* and I mourned. He also says, *"there is a time for dancing," "there is a time for laughing," "there is a time to live."* Yet, when you are deeply wounded by trauma, it can prove difficult to find a reason to dance, laugh or live. Often, it can be easier to simply wallow and get swallowed up in your pit of despair.

As Christians dealing with tribulation, we hope that we will face it with the grace of Job, the quintessential testament of a man of unwavering faith and trust in God despite his most unfavorable circumstances. Job was a man who had everything when suddenly, it was all taken from him, including the tragic death of his children. In just one day, Job received a series of negative reports as he learned of the loss of his livestock, the death of his servants and finally, the untimely departure of his children who were all crushed when a windstorm blew down the house in which they were celebrating leaving no survivors in its wake (Job 1). In his season of inconceivable grief, Job found the strength to still bless God by declaring *"the Lord gives, and the Lord takes away [BUT] Blessed be the name of the Lord."* Job 1:21 (NASB).

We hope that when we are abruptly stripped of everything we believe belonged to us, we can still acknowledge God's exceeding capacity for greatness. But, that will not always be our reality. Sometimes, we will become bitter and cold. We will slip into darkness and abandon faith. Sometimes, we will scream and we will shout. We will distance ourselves from God and fail to find purpose in living.

When I first saw the confirmation of pregnancy, I instantly became a mom. The sex of my child or how far along I was were inconsequential. I knew my child was within me, growing and becoming all that God created him or her to be, and I knew I was his or her mother. I identified with the word *mom* immediately. The title now belonged to me. Becoming a mom brought about a new and even greater purpose. However, after losing my angels, I felt completely stripped of that purpose and I lost myself. I wrestled with balancing fear and faith, with acknowledging identity and purpose, with fighting depression and finding conviction to live. I began to feel alone and ugly. I was gripped with shame as I believed that my body had failed me, failed us. And I had the scars to serve as a constant reminder—mental and physical.

By God's grace, I found freedom in my new normal. I found my breath. I also found my way to dance. Some tragedies will leave you with permanent scars that may serve to paralyze you, to limit your mobility. But in time, you can begin to remove the bondage of despair and find your dance. You can regain your laughter and joy. You can live. You can find your happily angel after.

I am exposing my heart and journey in this book in hopes of encouraging someone whose response to trauma has been less than perfect, less like Job. You have questioned your worth and lost your perspective. You are fighting to remember who you are and find the strength to stand under the pressure of your challenges. You cannot see the good or your God and you are losing courage. You cannot find a reason to live and you are desperately in need of some good news. But, your story does not have to end right there. You can rise out of your pit. You can overcome depression and discouragement. You can allow the grace of God to give you renewed perspective as you continue pushing towards destiny despite tribulation. If you muster up enough strength to take that next breath, you can also find your time to not only live, but to dance again.

Angel Taylor

Ugly

You stared in awe of your body just a week ago. In awe of your belly growing increasingly rounder. In awe of your body getting fuller with purpose. In awe of the promise you saw staring back at you from your full-length bedroom mirror as you closely examined your naked body. You saw the bump of hope developing. You saw destiny swelling up. You saw the fullness of life blossoming. And now, it is painful to even glance at. That body. With its flattened belly. With its engorgement—full of milk purposed to nurture a baby that is no longer here. Now, you avoid mirrors except in rare moments to take a peek in hopes of finding something good left in it.

The silence is too much to bear because you know all you will be left with are your thoughts. And your thoughts only drift and transport you to the times where you were filled with joy as you prepare for and anticipate the day when you will meet your beautiful baby for the first time. To a time of expectancy confirmed by an ever-expanding belly. To a time that the ultrasounds show you nothing but life as you see your baby grow and move. Now, the silence forces you to confront your new reality—that once expanding belly is now deflated and life no longer resides there.

After months of expectancy and anticipation, nothing could have prepared you for that day when the doctor performs an ultrasound then looks you square in the face to say, "Something is wrong with your baby and it will not live." At first, you freeze. Your heart sinks. You cannot speak. You attempt to comprehend the magnitude of her statement. It is so matter-of-fact. You begin to question yourself and her, what happened? Then, you tell yourself that it is not true. You hope, pray, and believe that the doctor has it wrong. You remember how pure and perfect your angel appeared in the prior ultrasounds. You remember how blessed you felt every time you stared in your full-length bedroom mirror. As your heart continues to sink within you, you remember your baby's strong and steady heartbeats and you remind yourself of God's greatness. No. The doctor is wrong. You will bring home this beautiful bundle of joy and she will be perfectly healthy. She will live. She will not die.

Yet, two weeks later when you go for another appointment, your worst fear becomes reality. The doctor's pronouncement about the miracle growing in your belly becomes true. Your baby no longer has a heartbeat. Your belly is still filled but there is no sign of life. The bump is still there but the growing miracle in your body can no longer be detected. Your entire world collapses. Your heart begins to ache and burst inside of you. You feel as if someone took a hammer to your life as to shatter it as if it were that full-length mirror. However, you do not cry. You do not speak. You just lie there, staring at the ultrasound screen, in pieces.

Vibrant

Upon approaching our second year of marriage, my husband and I decided that we were ready to expand our family. We decided to leave it in God's hands as to the perfect time. Initially, I did not experience any changes. But, after a while, I knew it was time to take a pregnancy test. I did it early in the morning before my husband had awakened so that I could surprise him if I was and so as not to disappoint him if I was not yet. I waited in anticipation for the test to confirm what I already felt. Moments later, the double lines burst forth from the pregnancy test without equivocation.

I could barely contain my excitement as I quickly walked back into our bedroom and woke Keven. I suggested that we go to our prayer room for our usual morning devotional. Without question, Keven arose and began a slow stumble towards the living room and then into the guest bedroom. I had placed the pregnancy test in a random page of the Bible and I asked him to read the morning scripture.

Still groggy, he began to open the Bible and saw the stick. His eyes stretched wide as if to force complete alertness. Keven looked at me and then he quickly looked back at the test. He glanced at me again briefly and then again in the Bible at the test. Now alert and wide awake, he asked "is this what I think it is?!" I nodded in affirmation and he excitedly grabbed me. We hugged. We kissed. We rejoiced. We were going to be parents!

We were so excited and thankful. I could not help but to thank God for honoring us with this new designation and purpose - parents. I became mom, Keven became dad and our precious child was growing within me.

Giddy

    I cannot overstate the joy I felt knowing there was a constant miracle being performed inside of me. God chose us to bring a little being into the world, to love and to raise. What a tremendous honor! I was so grateful that He thought enough of me to allow me to be the carrier of this child of purpose.

    When the high of our enthusiasm slightly diminished, I immediately set an appointment to meet with an OB/GYN. I did not know how far along I was, but I knew I needed to ensure I was getting the best prenatal treatment. Our miracle was growing in my body and I felt so far behind already. I needed to sleep well, to modify my diet, to accommodate this developing life within me. We were both committed to doing everything in our power to ensure our baby was healthy and strong.

    We took the day off to meet with the doctor. The urine test confirmed what we already knew. But, I also had to get some blood work taken. We were giddy with joy as we were able to see our baby for the first time. God says that children are a gift from above. Now, our hidden treasure, our gift from God, was so tangible as we stared in awe of our baby on the ultrasound screen. The heartbeat was palpable and strong. Our little nugget. The doctor expressed nearly as much enthusiasm as us and speculated that I was about six weeks along but would have a better idea once she received the results from my blood test.

It was nearing Father's Day weekend, so we thought it was a perfect time to surprise my parents with our arrival to their home in Georgia and share the great news of the upcoming arrival of our little one— their grandbaby. Shortly after leaving the doctor's office, we began our journey from Miami, Florida to Georgia. However, because of the intense excitement experienced in the last several days, working diligently and continuously prior to that, and the new bundle of joy growing in my belly, we were only able to drive about ninety minutes before needing to turn around. It had been a long day and we both needed rest.

Instead, we announced our little one's upcoming arrival to my family in Georgia via video chat as we drove back to visit Keven's family in Miami to share the news and reveal to them the sonogram. Everyone was elated for a new addition to the family. Our family was expanding and this time we were the ones adding to it. I had a miraculous treasure growing inside of me, a precious gem from God. Our lives would never be the same.

Mini

Our excitement, and the excitement of our families and friends, who were all now aware of my pregnancy, only increased over the course of the next several months. I had had several dreams about a baby girl and believed that I was carrying a girl. However, when it was time for the anatomy scan, our little one would not cooperate. Our baby continued to stay low in the uterus, curled into a ball. Even with prodding from the technician, our little one was not interested in revealing the sex. Already stubborn like daddy.

A few weeks later, at a second attempt to complete the anatomy scan, our baby decided to cooperate briefly before returning to the comfortable, curled position. We were having a girl! A baby girl! I already knew she was going to be spoiled and daddy's little princess. I could immediately see the beautiful ribbons in her hair, her tiny outfits, her cute little shoes and socks. We were having a girl! Keven was equally excited as he had also suspected we were having a girl. We decided to celebrate the news by going straight to the store to purchase her some pretty, little clothes. I was so excited; I was going to have a mini-me.

We would raise her to know that she was loved, she had purpose and a destiny, she was our little princess. We were so thrilled about this new journey as parents and could not wait for our baby girl to make her debut into our world. I just knew she was destined for greatness. She would be intelligent and fearless. We were so thrilled about this new journey that we were about to embark upon. Out of all the titles that we could have, "mommy" and "daddy" were the ones that we would be the proudest.

Special

It was our two-year anniversary when the perinatologist called me and said it was urgent that we come in to go over the results of my bloodwork. The initial results were fine but further testing indicated that there may be an issue with our baby girl. Keven and I went to her office immediately. Upon arrival, she informed us that our baby girl would likely have down syndrome. Some of the levels were abnormal which strongly indicated that something was wrong.

It was not the end of the world, I thought, but definitely not news that any first-time parents would care to hear. I had significantly worked with special needs children in the past and found them to be a joy. For three consecutive summers while in college, I volunteered at a special needs camp whose mission was to create an inclusive experience for children with special needs. It was some of the most meaningful and rewarding work that I even considered becoming a special needs teacher. Of course, I knew that being a parent to a special-needs child would present several challenges, but it would be okay. We would be ok. I knew enough about God to know that he could heal our baby girl but even if He did not, He could give us the grace to properly care for and raise our child of purpose. The doctor gave us the option to consider an abortion and we immediately declined. We both agreed abortion was absolutely not an option for us and did not align with our faith.

After leaving the doctor's office, we tried to make the best of the rest of our anniversary day. We went out to eat, took pictures of my growing belly and just enjoyed each other's company. I began researching the indicators that the doctor had mentioned once we were settled in for the evening. I came across several blogs and vlogs that stated that they had been told the same about their child while in utero and their child did not have down syndrome or any health issues for that matter. I was encouraged and began thinking that the doctor probably had it wrong. She would be perfectly healthy. Eventually, I pushed the doctor's concerns out of my mind. We prayed for and continued to anticipate the impending arrival of our healthy baby girl.

A Time to Pray

Neither of us would accept the doctor's concern about our baby girl. We rejected it and continued in our excitement and planning for her arrival. However, a few weeks later, I had another ultrasound. This appointment completely upended our world. We were able to see our baby girl and her heartbeat, which was still very strong and steady. But, the technician was clearly concerned by what she was seeing on the screen. She did not say anything to us but continued the examination and then went to speak with the doctor. The doctor came into the room and performed her own ultrasound. Then she looked directly at us, before focusing her attention on me, and told us that our baby will die, whether it is before birth or shortly after she is born, she would not survive.

Keven and I were completely shocked and baffled. We could barely speak. The doctor continued and stated that the issue was not down syndrome as they had initially thought. She did not know why, but our baby girl had severe intra-uterine growth restriction. It was as if she had completely stopped growing and was measuring three or four weeks behind where she should be at that point, and there was no medical explanation for it.

It was not so easy to reject what the doctor was saying this time. She was so straightforward and matter-of-fact. She referred us to a pediatric cardiologist for a fetal echo for further examination. Although shocked, we attempted to maintain hope. We continued to pray and declare that the doctor had it wrong. Our baby girl would experience a growth spurt and baffle the doctors. We prayed vigorously. She will live and not die.

Dim

The appointment with the pediatric cardiologist was a few days later. The technician and cardiologist examined our baby girl's heart and did a thorough examination of the uterus. Neither could pinpoint exactly what was wrong but were able to see that something was indeed wrong. One major area in her heart seemed to be lacking proper blood flow. The cardiologist did not say much but instructed us to come back in a couple of weeks. He said it would be easier to see once she had grown a bit bigger.

We left the office feeling concerned but decided we would not let it get us down. We encouraged ourselves and spoke positively. We continued to pray and declare the good health and restoration for our baby girl. We prayed and believed that the doctors were mistaken, and our baby girl would prove them all wrong. Not that we do not appreciate the advice and expertise of medical professionals. But, we simply chose to exercise our faith and believe for a miracle for our Angel. We do believe that the medical professionals present facts, but we also believe God has the final say and has the capacity to work wonders despite the facts. We prayed for a miracle.

Although I continued to profess declarations over our baby girl, rejecting the pronouncement of the doctor, praying over her little limbs, her bones, her organs, this time, I was not completely convinced that the doctor was wrong. But, maybe it was just a test of our faith. God, we completely trust you. She would be a miracle baby.

Gray

We went back to the cardiologist on a Monday, a couple of weeks later, and learned that our Angel no longer had a heartbeat. As predicted, we lost our baby. I looked closely at the screen as the cardiologist performed the ultrasound. What had been so normal to our eyes for six months was no longer there. Our baby's strong and rapid heartbeat had vanished. There was no sound. There was no activity to indicate life. No movement at all. Angel's body was still visible. Floating in amniotic fluid. But she was no longer.

Although the perinatologist had already warned us that it would happen, it did not make the news any less shocking or painful when it did. I felt as if my heart was ripped out of my body and a huge lump had developed in my throat. I felt as if the room was spinning as I tried to comprehend what I was seeing. It was all surreal in the worst kind of way.

The cardiologist and technician both expressed their condolences and sent us on our way. It was as if I was in a haze, completely numb and in disbelief. I could not even cry, I was so in shock. What happened to the life that was growing in my belly? I have carried this baby for six months. There is no way she is gone just like that.

Keven hugged and comforted me for a few minutes before we got in the car to leave. All I could think was that God was testing us. We had another appointment for the next day at the OB/GYN. We would see the heartbeat then. Everything is okay, and the baby will be fine. I had to hold on to the hope that what we were seeing was false. Our baby girl would be restored and this would be a part of her testimony, our testimony. Our baby girl will show them. Things would be fine. I fought to hold on to my faith.

A Time to Weep

    Keven was in prayer, confessing and declaring over our baby all day and partway through the night. But I could barely speak. I hoped and I tried to believe but I could not find the right words to say to God. I imagined that I was being punished, that I have reaped what I sowed in some fashion, but what? What did I do that was so horrible that could possibly reap something so devastating? The death of our first child after carrying her for six months. I know that I am not perfect, but I try to live a life pleasing to God. Yes, there were plenty of missteps, but I believed I was in right standing with our Father. How could He let this happen to us? Although I heard it clear as day, "This is not a punishment. You are not being punished," I could not shake the feeling. Even a couple of months afterwards, though it offered me some reassurance, I still had moments where I thought I must be suffering the consequences of some heinous sin I had committed. But, what?

    At our OB-GYN appointment the next day, we insisted that she perform another ultrasound. She agreed. We examined closely but nothing changed. Our baby still has no heartbeat. She tells us that I will need to decide when I want to be induced so that they can deliver the baby. She knows it is a lot for us to accept and process and tells us to give her a call once we have had an opportunity to discuss and have decided what we want to do. She also states that we cannot wait long, though, as it could be toxic to my body to continue to carry this baby that has passed. We listen, and we leave.

We are silent as we walk back to the car. We have no words. We are heavy. Keven begins to drive but then pulls over into an empty parking lot. He convinces me to get into the back seat and he holds me. We both cry but are mostly silent. Heavy. Hurt. Eventually, Keven encourages me to call my mom.

It is as if what has happened suddenly hit me. I completely break down and cannot control my sobs. I am heartbroken and devastated. I look down at my belly that is home to our now lifeless baby. All I can think is what happened? Why did our baby girl have to leave us? Why are we here left with so much pain? What did we do to deserve this?

I do not know how long we sat in that parking lot while I wept, but Keven holds me until I am able to speak somewhat clearly through my tears. He calls my mom and passes me the phone. I tell her the news. She expresses how much she loves me and how much her and my dad have been praying for us and the baby. She offers some encouraging words. I tell her that we have decided not to wait to have our Angel and that I would be induced the next day. We have already called the hospital and scheduled our appointment to deliver our Angel.

Later, I find out that her and my dad are on a layover and will be with us in a few short hours. She did not even tell me they were coming but it meant the world to me that my parents would drop everything to make sure their baby girl and son in law had the support we needed during this terrible time. It was a relief to have my parents near to comfort me during the worst time I have ever had to endure in my life.

After I hung up with my mom, I insisted that we go back to our office. I tried to distract myself with work and not think about what has occurred and what I may expect for the next day. But my emotions get the best of me. I cannot stop crying. I research the induction and delivery process and then try to lie down and rest. But my mind continues to race. So many thoughts flood my mind and I am unable to turn it off. I beg and plead with the Lord, let it not be true. Let our baby's heartbeat return with no adverse effect from the hours of deprivation. I cried and pleaded with the Lord but deep down I knew that she was gone. But we could not give up. God is a miracle worker and He can do it! We prayed all day. Finally, around 10pm, I decided to attempt sleep.

Surprisingly, I fell asleep almost immediately. But a few hours later, I wake up abruptly, my whole body shaking and crying hysterically. I cannot bear the thought of having to give birth and not bring our baby home. Ever. I do not know how long I cried but eventually I fell back asleep until my alarm woke me up around 4am. It was time.

Still

It was as if I was in a daze as I dressed myself and prepared to go to the hospital. My dad said a prayer before we left the house. As Keven drove, my parents followed closely behind. There were no tears and few words as we made our way before sunrise. It was as if we were headed to a funeral—somber and still.

Although we already knew the outcome, Keven and I asked for another ultrasound. Maybe, God? I was cautiously optimistic as I saw something pulsing in the corner of the screen and asked the technician what it was. Any hope that remained was dashed as she explained that it was just one of my vessels pumping blood. Our baby girl was gone. It was confirmed for the third time.

The nurse explained to me how the medication would be used to induce my labor. It cannot be used for a live birth as it is harmful to the fetus. However, since our baby girl was a stillbirth, it did not matter as it was only me that they needed to be concerned with. The gravity of what I was about to experience pierced me deeply. But I could not cry anymore. I was numb.

My parents stayed for a few hours as we waited for my cervix to dilate. The days in the hospital were different than the day that we found out. Although still somewhat somber, there was inexplicable peace. We were still able to have some light-hearted conversations and enjoy each other's company. We continued to wait in the still quietness of the room in which I would give birth to our Angel.

A Time to Release

Keven and I were left alone in the hospital room as time progressed. He was keeping everyone updated via text. My labor advanced and I began to feel slight contractions. The contractions began to increase and I knew that it was almost time. The labor and delivery were relatively painless and easy. Effortless and without assistance. I did not know what to think or do. I called the nurse, who had just left the room moments before, to let her know that our baby was here.

Our nurse gave us time to decide whether we would like to see or hold our baby girl. She would clean her up for us. She took our Angel to clean her up and get her pictures taken and for hand and footprints. The hospital offers it complimentary for grieving mothers, to keep a piece of their precious angel. We were able to see the tiny hand and footprints—evidence of our once developing and life-filled baby. To date, we have not retrieved the complimentary pictures.

Nurses are the real heroes. I know that our nurses were a Godsend as they made the transition of our Angel much smoother than we could have ever imagined. Each one of them hold a special place in my heart because of the kindness and compassion they showed to us. Because my induced labor was over the course of two days, I had three nurses--one there to take care of me prior to Angel's birth, one during and one after Angel's birth. Each of them were so special and compassionate. Words truly cannot express how grateful I am to each of them.

Susanne, with her calming demeanor and charismatic personality. Christine, with her sensitivity and attentive care. Rachel, with her larger than life personality and sense of humor. Each was perfect for the stage in which they were a part of our lives.

After a stressful day and hysterical night, it was a relief to have such a beautiful birthing process even in the midst of the heartache. God was truly with us, through the presence of His Holy Spirit and through each of our nurses. We could not have been more thankful.

Pink

Ultimately, Keven and I decided not to see or hold Angel's body. We had experienced enough trauma. We did not want the sight of her lifeless body forever imprinted in our memories. We only wanted to remember her life as she grew and expanded my belly. Our beautiful princess. Our blooming miracle.

Shortly after delivery, we were informed by a nurse that we needed to make funeral arrangements for our Angel. The thought was gripping. From delivery to funeral arrangements so suddenly. Everything was moving so quickly. We were provided with a list of funeral home options nearby. Keven agreed to review the list and make the calls. While making the calls, I watched him. I saw a glimpse of his heart ache. He had sadness in his eyes and pain in his voice. I identified with it. What was going on with us. This had to be a dream.

Within a couple of days, we both went to the funeral home we selected. We both became overwhelmed with the idea of planning a funeral and burying our beloved Angel. We decided to have her lifeless body cremated. Our Angel, her spirit had already left us to be with the Father. We selected a pretty pink urn for what remained of her. We signed the necessary documents to allow the hospital to release her body for cremation. We were forced to say goodbye.

A Time to Cope

One of the hardest parts of grieving is attempting to navigate engaging people in conversation about your recent loss. How do you properly and graciously respond to people, including family and friends, that inquire about your uterus or make truly insensitive statements although they mean well? *"Do not worry, it will happen when it is time." "I know exactly how you feel, I had a miscarriage when I was seven weeks along." "So many people lose children, you all will be fine." "When are you all going to try again?"* How do they expect me to respond to those types of questions?

What do you say to strangers who ask when you and your husband will have children? "*You're still young so y'all should go ahead and have children.*" This just a few weeks after losing and having to make funeral arrangements for your first child. And while you politely respond because of the innocence of the questions, you really want to just scream. You also want to hide. Maybe it is best to completely disconnect rather than deal with the pain of continuing to be polite or blow up on someone.

The profound pain of losing a child, regardless of stage, cannot be overstated. Being the bearer of such a gift, it is only natural to get immediately attached regardless of how many weeks you advance. The very day the double lines appeared on my pregnancy stick, I became mom. You have already learned to love unconditionally this being that you have never even met. You have already determined that you will do everything in your power to ensure that this child will have the best in life. Something immediately changes within you.

Because our Angel passed away after 20 weeks, I had to experience the pains of labor and delivery. Although the physical pain was light and manageable, having delivered her and knowing for some time that her lifeless body rested in the corner of our room, adds an extra layer of emotional pain. Our loss is compounded with having to labor and deliver a baby knowing she was no longer there. Knowing she will never get to achieve all we had hoped she would accomplish. Knowing she would never reach the destiny we had imagined for her.

With each stage, we loved our Angel more passionately. Now it appears those stages bring deeper heart-wrenching pain. Articulating that to those who have not been there has proven difficult. But I am most grateful for those who have reached out to simply show love. They may not have walked in our shoes, and they know they cannot relate to my exact circumstances, but they know pain. They know trauma and relate. They listen and have loved me through.

Empty

I want to pray and to cry out to God but I am afraid that He will not answer. I want to know why but I am sure I will never know the answer. Although, it is likely this will never happen again, even the doctors stated as much, I am frightened that it will. As much as I want us to have children, this is in the back of my mind, really the forefront. What if it does happen again? How will I even manage this again?

Surely, there is no way God would allow us to go through this again. He is a merciful and gracious God. He knows that is too much for any person to bear. But what if...? Despite what I tell myself to be hopeful and encouraged, I cannot help but to continue to think what if.

The greatest gift that could have come from this deep pain and one of the few things that gives me solace is the fact that my connectedness and love for my husband has grown exponentially. I did not realize how much deeper I could love him. But having him by my side, grieving and mourning with me, being strong for me in those times when I just could not deal, caring for me and just loving me harder, has given me a greater appreciation for God for creating him just for me. During this time, I often find myself feeling lost and alone if he is not near. I would rather just sleep than be left alone with my thoughts--hoping it will numb the pain or cause it to dissipate completely. Maybe when I wake up, I will feel better. But that is almost never the case. I toss and I turn and never truly feel refreshed. I am merely existing now, feeling as if I have been stripped of my purpose and passion.

A Time to Mourn

I had taken a few weeks to mourn. Then I felt the urgency to get back to work. We could grieve, but God did not call us to be stagnant or at a complete standstill. We could get through. We had to fight. Fight, is what we did. We fought, and we pushed. Fought to get up every day and pushed through pain to connect with others. Eventually, we got into a steady routine. I felt as if we had conquered our grief and I was on the road to finding happiness in our new normal.

But, it became obvious that I did not take the time to properly mourn. I was a mess. I was moody and would still cry uncontrollably on a regular basis. One day, I was unable to stop the tears from pouring and decided that I may need professional help. Though I had never needed it in the past, I believe mental health is a topic that warrants critical attention and I am a huge proponent of seeking counseling when necessary. I sought a Christian counselor whom I felt could assist me in navigating my emotions and my now fragile faith. I went to visit her that very day.

Counseling was exactly what I needed. I was able to vent and to cry and to express my fears and anxiety without feeling as if I was unloading or unduly burdening anyone else. Because my husband was also grieving, I never wanted to overburden him with the full magnitude of my thoughts and feelings. I did not want him to be too overwhelmed dealing with his own grief while constantly trying to comfort me as well. He needed to mourn, I needed the same and thought it inconsiderate for us to constantly dump on each other.

We needed professional help. I found it easier to speak to a third party who was licensed to handle issues such as mine.

      My therapist assisted me greatly, providing me with various coping mechanisms. She even allowed some open sessions so that Keven could join us and we benefit from grief counseling as a couple. To truly mourn, I had to confront my new reality and acknowledge that I was not okay with it. Our Angel left just as quickly as she had come and with her departure, the pieces of my life were too shattered to sort or mend on my own. Just as I was drowning in depression, my therapist helped me to begin to focus on the level ground. I began to see it. The pain and the heartache began to diminish with my renewed perspective and I slowly felt that I could eventually come up for air. I was finally on the road to recovery after Angel.

Michael Angel

Uncertain

We knew that this day would come but were unsure as to how soon. I partly wanted to get pregnant again right away while another part of me just wanted to wait and take our time. Just the thought of being pregnant filled me with anxiety. I knew that no matter if it happened immediately or five years later, I would experience a wave of emotions with my next pregnancy. Angel Taylor will never be forgotten. How giddy with joy we became when we learned of her existence. How proud and humbled we felt. The love that stirred as we contemplated her future. But then also the heart-wrenching pain that pulled us into the depths of sorrow after her loss. The fear and anxiety that followed. So, when that second line appeared on the pregnancy test, albeit faint, I had mixed emotions.

On one hand, I was excited that our little family was growing, again. But on the other hand, I was nervous and admittedly afraid as I considered worst-case scenarios. Surely nothing like that would ever happen again! The sudden departure of our Angel Taylor would not happen again. I tried to reassure myself. But the what ifs started to flood my mind, no matter how much I tried to reassure myself.

I did not want to get my hopes up just yet. God, this is all you because I cannot handle it on my own. Please, is all I could say. I was so sleepy before but now I cannot get my mind to stop racing. It was going to be a long next several months.

A Time to Believe

It is the night before my first ultrasound and what little excitement that may have been there gives way to more uneasiness and anxiety. I toss and turn all night, my mind racing. What if there really is no baby? What if my hormones are just elevated because of the recent loss? Yes, my period has not returned this month, but it is possible that it is just irregular and may be late. If there is a baby, what if there is no heartbeat? I am not experiencing any symptoms, not even the mild ones that I experienced with Angel. No tenderness and no unusual fatigue like before. That cannot be a good sign, right? I spend a restless night wrestling with my anxiety and doubt.

The time drags on until it is time for me to wake up and get ready. I still have some uneasiness, but I try to say a prayer to ease some of the anxiety. Later, Keven prays with me and that helps as well. Still a bit nervous but not as anxious as before. We speak with the doctor and express our concerns and ask all of the questions that we can think of. She is very patient with us---understanding our need for reassurance while also being cautious with her words. After all, there are no guarantees as we know far too well.

Now for the moment of truth. As I undress, Keven says another prayer before the doctor reenters the room. Standard testing then the ultrasound. And there we see it, as clear as day, the heartbeat. It is strong and rapid. All good signs at this stage of the pregnancy. At that moment, I breathe a sigh of relief and for the first time since learning of our pregnancy, I become overcome with excitement thinking of our little one to come. I allow my thoughts to quickly go there before being confronted with reality. Our Angel had a very strong heartbeat the entire time until her little heart just could not support her any longer. So, although a very good sign at this stage, we are not completely in the clear. But God is sovereign, and He is a gracious and merciful God. Surely, He would not allow us to experience anything like that again and especially not back to back. I am hopeful yet still trying not to get too attached to the idea.

    We also had the Panorama blood test that detects diseases or disabilities. I must admit that I am nervous. I keep telling myself that everything is fine and that the blood work will come back completely normal. And deep down I believe that is true. But I still cannot help but to think about the possibility that it is not. We were further along when we received the news about our Angel possibly having an abnormality. Of course, the tests are not 100% accurate so even if something may seem wrong, the baby may actually be perfectly normal and healthy and vice versa. But of course, my prayer is that the blood tests show no indication of anything wrong and that indeed there is nothing wrong. We will have a perfectly, healthy baby this time.

Light

When we learned the forecasted due date of our baby, we were so amazed. We just knew that it was a sign from the Lord that all was well. We initially received the bad news of our Angel on our anniversary last year. Now, our baby's expected due date was our anniversary for the following year. So, if all went well, we would be having our baby on or right around our anniversary. This was encouraging news.

Our rainbow baby was here to make up for the pain that we endured losing our Angel. Our anniversary would once again be associated with a joyous memory as opposed to a negative one. God is so funny, and He really knows how to make things up to His children. It is the scripture come to life, *"Weeping may endure for a night, But joy comes in the morning."* (Psalm 30:5, NKJV). Our morning is on the horizon and we feel so blessed.

Low

It was the day after my first appointment when I received a call from the doctor's office. When I saw the name on my caller ID, my heart dropped. I knew it was too soon for them to be reminding me of my next appointment. I picked up the phone with complete dread expecting the worst. The nurse said congratulations, confirming my pregnancy. And then the news. My progesterone levels were low and the doctor is prescribing me pills to increase it. In speaking with her, I learned that low progesterone could possibly lead to a miscarriage. She did not say it in so many words, but I could read between the lines. I asked so many questions and although she was so sweet and patient, I could not help but to think that this was possibly the reason I lost Angel.

Maybe because I initially started out with a different doctor whose office took my blood and then did not submit the results to my new doctor for several weeks, that it was missed. My eyes overflowed with tears and I grieved for my Angel. She could still be here with us. Because Keven was with clients, I waited to tell him about the call and instead called my mom. I was driving and could not do the research I wanted to learn more about this progesterone I was prescribed. I asked my mom about it and she reassured me. I shared my suspicions about us losing Angel and how it possibly could have been avoided. But she said that God knew even if the doctors did not catch it and if it was His will, He would have saved Angel. Just know that God is in control and He has the final say despite the doctors. There was a purpose in our Angel leaving us.

    Although I could not completely shake the feeling, I felt some reassurance after speaking with her. I picked up my prescription later that day and began taking it as prescribed. I would do whatever was necessary to ensure a healthy pregnancy this time.

A Time to Declare

It seems like it has been forever since our last appointment, especially given that we had appointments for Angel nearly every other week. I have gotten excited and am very optimistic about this pregnancy. My husband and I will be parents this year and will experience no additional losses. Our baby will be perfect and healthy with no challenges or disabilities. This will be the perfect pregnancy. We both believe it.

But as we get closer to our next appointment, the anxiety starts to creep in and old thoughts begin flooding back. Instead of getting caught up in and running away with my thoughts, I begin to make declarations over my womb, over our child. I speak God's truth. To further increase my faith and help to solidify my declarations, I listen to the audible book I had recently purchased. One of my best friends recommended it to me. It is entitled "Supernatural Childbirth" by Jackie Mizer.

Towards the end of the book, the author references several scriptures that speak to my heart about the life I am carrying. She then ends it with declarations for those dealing with infertility and barrenness, pregnancy and pregnancy symptoms, and childbirth. This helps to bring me back to a place of peace, excitement, and optimism concerning my pregnancy and our impending parenthood.

Bright

Though I can say that now, nearly five months after we lost our Angel, I have more peace, more joy, and happiness, I doubt I will be completely at ease until we bring our healthy, perfect baby into the world and are able to hold our baby in our arms. As my pregnancy progresses, I have less anxiety and doubt though. We continue to pray and make declarations over our baby which has been helping to ease the apprehension. But I would be lying if I said that it was completely gone.

I continue to have flashbacks to when I was pregnant with Angel and when the doctors first expressed some concern. I remembered when one told us point blank that she would not live, whether she did not survive through term or whether I bring her to term and she die shortly after giving birth to her. Our Angel would not live. Such a pronouncement is impossible to forget. It comes back from time to time during this pregnancy. But every ultrasound that we have had at this point shows a lively and active baby. Full of life and energy which fills my husband and me with optimism.

They were unable to get any results from the blood samples I had given them for the panorama test. This test checks for specific chromosomal issues and certain birth defects. It also by default can determine the gender of your child earlier than what an ultrasound can see. When my doctor called me to let me know I would need to give more blood, I was nervous and crazy thoughts began rushing through my mind about whether my baby was going to be ok. But she reassured us that there was no problem, sometimes it is just too early for the test to detect fetal cells within the blood. That mostly eased my mind, but I was still slightly anxious. We had been looking forward to the results for a couple of weeks at that point and now had to wait another 7-10 days.

At my next appointment, our nurse greeted us excitedly and jokingly stating that she had tried to call but I did not answer the phone, so we would have to wait for the doctor to come back with the report. After she left, Keven and I smiled at each other knowing it could only be good news by the cheery way that the nurse interacted with us. The doctor only further confirmed our suspicions when she entered the room with a bright smile. She immediately gave us the report that our baby was doing well and that we were at low risk for chromosomal issues. She also told us that we were having a boy!

Keven and I were grinning from ear to ear with the results and I was finally able to exhale a sigh of relief. After we finished, it felt as if Keven and I floated out of the office. Neither of us could stop smiling and hugging each other. We both even teared up a bit because we were just so happy realizing that it was around this time before that the doctors expressed some concern about our Angel. Now, here we are in almost the same exact place in our second pregnancy and we have nothing but good reports. We cannot help but rejoice and immediately share the news with family and close friends. A weight has been lifted and we no longer have to go to our appointments with bated breath. God confirmed through the doctors and these tests that this indeed is a healthy pregnancy and we would bring a healthy baby boy into this world, this year.

Expectant

Here I am at 17 weeks and I am still not sure whether I feel baby moving. Because I am always reading about babies, particularly other people's stories, I knew some first-time mothers who started feeling flutters at 15 weeks and lots of mothers saying how much they love being able to feel their baby move now at 17 weeks. I know that it may be hard to tell until I get a bit further along and that this is not outside the norm. But it does make me nervous. I never truly felt Angel move, even up to the 24 weeks that I carried her. So not feeling any recognizable movement yet is making me recount my experience with our Angel baby. I wish I could get an ultrasound every day just to see my little prince move. I must trust that God has everything under control.

Little

We had the anatomy scan of our baby boy on March 31. I was always so eager to see him again. I have now been feeling him for weeks, so just to be able to see him on screen again was thrilling. He is an extremely active baby, which is such a relief. So different from my experience with Angel. To this day, I cannot say definitively that I ever felt her move. At least, no recognizable movement. To feel how our baby boy moves and responds to his daddy's voice is so exhilarating. I welcome his activity. I know people say once he is bigger, I will not be as excited about it, but it is such a reassurance to me that everything is going well and that he is developing as he should, that I do not think I will ever mind. It is a sign of life and I love it!

At the anatomy scan, we were able to see everything. The tech talked us through what she was looking at and said that all looked well. However, due to our history of IUGR and stillbirth, she expressed some concern about him being a little bit behind in his growth. Initially I was not worried, because she said he was 10 ounces, which according to most baby measurements, is right about where he should be at 20 weeks. She had us speak to the doctor anyways and he listed some things that could be the cause, none that he felt were our situation. But, just like the tech, he said the only reason for the concern is because of our history. He mentioned that they would monitor our baby's growth more closely and once the baby is viable to live outside the womb on his own, if they felt it necessary, they would take him. He said maybe as early as 24 weeks. We listened patiently, but Keven and I immediately rejected that idea.

Our baby would continue to develop and grow to term--he will not be premature, and I will have a natural childbirth, no need for them to induce me. Given that they can never truly pinpoint a conception date and previous visits already had him measuring about 4-5 days smaller than our due date, the doctor said he actually seemed to only be measuring 3 days behind as opposed to the week that he initially thought. After some other expressed concerns and what they would need to do moving forward, the doctor prescribed us to get a fetal echo just to be sure. And we left.

Initially we were both unfazed by the concern because we know what God had already spoken over our son and that we will indeed bring him into this earth and raise him as a child of the Most High. However, I cannot say that everything since then has been all roses. Keven seems to be just fine, but I have begun to worry that something may be wrong with our son. I try to dismiss the thoughts and continue to declare wholeness and health and growth and perfect development, etc. But after reading and seeing where some others say their babies are at 20 weeks, I feel a bit of concern. All I can do is pray and continue to declare over my child, my womb and my own mind. Everything will be just fine when they do the fetal EKG and they will see that he is growing perfectly healthy and strong and that his growth is on par with where he should be. Now to just keep those worrisome thoughts under submission as we wait the two weeks for our next appointments.

A Time to Hear

I am in week 23 and I must admit that I am a bit anxious. This is about the time that we lost our Angel though we did not find out until a few days later, after we had reached the 24-week mark. I know that everything is good with our little prince, but I cannot wait to get over this hump. The fetal EKG did not show anything too concerning and our baby boy was still doing very well and as active as ever. But, I still had not totally conquered my thoughts.

It was Friday evening and while my husband was out, I decided to take a nap. We were both so tired so when I finally woke up, I saw that my husband had come in to nap as well. I tried to be as quiet as possible getting up to use the restroom. He does not sleep much so when he does, I try my best not to disturb him. But when I went to the bathroom, I kept sniffling because my nose was running. Nothing new or a cause for concern because I am always congested these days. Except when I went to blow my nose, a huge blood clot came out. Based on previous research, I knew that some women tend to have more nosebleeds during pregnancy and there was really no reason to be concerned. Which was no different for me. I never experienced a nose bleed until I was pregnant with Angel. In my 23rd week. Right before we found out that we had lost her.

Although normally I knew it should not cause me to worry, all of the memories from that experience came flooding back. I remembered waking up from my nap and my nose started bleeding. We were both worried at the time until we researched it and learned it was fairly common and is not an indicator that something may be wrong with the baby. So that appeased us and eased our minds. However, three days later we found out that our Angel no longer had a heartbeat. This time, I was trying not to panic despite the research. I remained in the bathroom trying to decide whether I should tell my husband or just allow my nose to clot and remain calm. I began praying and crying unable to allow the positive thoughts to remain. After about 10 minutes, I woke up my husband with my concern. jo

    He tried to reassure me but then stated that maybe we should go to the hospital, so I can have peace of mind. At first, I was like no I am just being silly. The last time I had a nosebleed was because I got too hot while I was napping. I usually turn on the fan or lower the temperature of the air conditioner when I lie down. But just like the time with Angel, I did neither. My husband reminded me of that fact as well. I decided I would just eat, give our prince some time to wake up and become active as he usually is. However, as I ate and drank cold water, I still felt no movement. I tried shaking him and still nothing. I realized that I could not remember the last time I had felt him...maybe earlier that morning. Naturally, I became even more concerned.

    Keven urged me to get dressed so we could go to the ER to have our baby checked. I tried so hard to stay calm and mostly succeeded but tears began rolling down my face as we drove to the hospital. Keven prayed and reassured me that everything was ok. When we got to the ER, I told the nurses my history and they understood my fear and concern. They then checked our baby's heartbeat which was loud and clear and rapid as it should be. As soon as I heard the first beat, my eyes filled with tears. Tears of joy this time.

They then hooked me up to a heart rate monitor that could also detect movement. We were able to hear the baby's heart and movement even when I could not feel every movement that he made. Because of my initial uneasiness and history, they left us there for about an hour and all I could do was thank God and smile listening to our baby. There is nothing like having peace of mind. Keven knew everything was ok but preferred that we make the trip just so that I would have the same reassurance. And now I did.

Pain

  I made it past the hump. What I call the Angel hump. We got past week 24 and all seemed to be going well. We could breathe a sigh of relief. The doctors said he was a bit small but still within range. We continued to pray and declare his healthiness and that he would go to full term without complications.

  Our next appointment after the hump was May 12. With only a few minor concerns along the way, we did not expect this appointment to be any different than the others of our little prince. However, when we looked at the screen of the ultrasound, it looked markedly different. Our son looked perfectly fine and his usual active self. But the womb looked smaller. After finishing her exam, the technician stated that the amniotic fluid was significantly low, considerably lower than it had been just a few weeks prior. She had to speak to the doctor about his recommendation. After speaking with him, she sent us home telling me to drink plenty of fluids, more than I am used to drinking, over the weekend and they would recheck my levels on Monday. If the levels did not improve, they would have to determine whether to deliver him early to prevent any issues from the low amniotic fluid. I was a little disheartened but resolved. I would do whatever it took to make sure our little one continued to thrive. Keven bought me gallons of water and I began our aim to increase amniotic fluid.

  But, the next morning, I awakened with severe pain in my neck, down my spine and in my knees. I could barely move. Keven was already awake and downstairs, so I had to call him by phone to assist me. He came up immediately and began lightly massaging my neck and back until the pain subsided. My knees continued to throb though much lighter than before. He massaged my knees and legs as well. I no longer had pain in my neck and back, but my knees persisted. The pain left enough for me to get up and attempt to walk. So, we walked. I kept thinking, "is this the joint pain that they refer to when pregnant? That escalated quickly!" Eventually I had to lie back down and tried icing my knees. It helped so long as the ice remained.

Then I remembered that many pregnant women use the pool to ease joint pain. We went to the neighborhood pool and I gave it a try. It was also a temporary fix. After leaving the pool, I decided to lie down and continue with the ice while Keven went to run some errands and go to the gym for a bit. Then, the ice stopped working. The pain became more and more unbearable until it was excruciating, and I could not walk without considerable effort. I called Keven. I did not want to go to the hospital, but I did not know what else to do to manage the pain. I could no longer withstand it, so we had to do something. Keven picked me up and we were off to the hospital.

When we arrived, the nurse took my vitals and blood and it was discovered that my white blood count was extremely high, indicating that my body was trying to fight something. With few pain crises growing up and my last one prior to this time being approximately 15 years ago, I was the model patient that had been diagnosed with sickle cell anemia. Because of my phenomenal health and rare hospitalizations, only my blood work indicated sickle cell anemia so many of my doctors were stunned with the diagnosis and always assumed that I may only have the trait. The pain in my knees finally indicated otherwise.

The doctor informed me that it was not the joint pain pregnant women experience but a pain crisis associated with sickle cell. He offered me pain killers and explained that they would not harm our baby. I usually try to do my own research before taking anything, but I was in so much pain. So, I took the painkillers. Because I was pregnant, they hooked a fetal heart rate monitor onto my belly. Throughout the night, our baby's heart rate began fluctuating drastically. Although my knee pain eventually subsided, they admitted me to keep an eye on him. It was time to watch and increase prayer.

Tested

"Happy Mother's Day!" The texts came flooding in. Many people, friends and family alike, were so excited about our son as they knew about our Angel. They were rooting for us. At that point, only my parents knew I was in the hospital, having been admitted the night before. The doctors continued to monitor the fetal heart rate and were concerned about the fluctuations. An ultrasound was ordered for the following morning to check the amniotic fluid levels. I was no longer in pain, but we were very concerned about our prince's heart rate. We tried not to panic but continued with the fluids.

I was receiving fluids via the IV but also trying to drink as much as I could bear, though I was not very thirsty. Keven tried to fill me with fluids, constantly bringing me drinks and encouraging me to continue drinking past my fill, hoping to increase the amniotic fluid levels. We should receive a good report the next day at the ultrasound.

The next day came and it was time for my ultrasound. The levels looked slightly more than they were the past Friday but still not nearly at the previous levels where it seemed like he was swimming in fluid. The technician confirmed that there was slightly more fluid but still not out of the danger zone. She asked me if I experienced any pain in my belly or had any bleeding. I told her no and mentioned the pain crisis. She just shook her head and asked us to wait while she got her supervisor to come take a look.

I did not think much of it as it seemed to be usual protocol for the tech to then get their supervisor or a doctor to review the results with him or her. The supervisor came back into the room and they discussed what they were seeing in hushed voices. The supervisor asked me as well had I experienced abdominal pain or bleeding. I once again denied either and inquired as to why. The technician thought maybe I had a placental abruption, but the supervisor did not think so. I did not have any symptoms of a placental abruption. They said they would share the results with my doctor to review and sent me back to my room.

My doctor decided to order another ultrasound for a couple of days later and continued to monitor the baby. She indicated that I may need to go to the main hospital with the more advanced NICU if the baby needed to be delivered. It was best that I be there already as opposed to possibly having to transport me and baby later. I decided to wait it out as I did not want to think of delivery and preferred to stay there while they monitored me.

The next few days were a blur. At one point, I began having a severe migraine, nothing that I had ever experienced before. I wanted to scream and holler but knew I could not. The nurse took my blood pressure and it was dangerously elevated. She stated that I was experiencing preeclampsia and needed to take something to assist with getting my blood pressure back to a normal range. Another ultrasound was taken but the technician, a different one than the days prior, stated that he did not see any sort of placental abruption. He dismissed the idea altogether and encouraged us that everything was fine. He did state that the levels were still low but there was no abruption.

After some time of monitoring, I finally agreed to allow them to transport me to the main hospital. I still was not completely comfortable with the idea of possibly delivering our baby soon. But, just in case. We continued to pray and decree positive outcomes and no adverse effects would occur from the low fluid. Once I was settled in my new hospital room, the nurses began to check me.

One of the nurses suspected that something was wrong because of my hyper-sensitive reflexes and took my blood pressure once again. My blood pressure was even higher than it had been before when I was experiencing the severe migraine. She wrapped the rails of the bed in padding because it was a possibility that I could have a seizure with my pressure being that high. I knew I was in for an extended stay but prayed our little prince would be fine.

Detached

We were introduced to a specialist/perinatologist who my OB/GYN thought would be helpful in monitoring me and the baby. We spoke about my history, my anxiety, and what had been occurring within the past several days that brought me into the hospital. Afterwards, she said she was leaving to go home but would come back to check on me when she would be back at work the next day. Keven and I had an immediate connection with her and agreed that she would be my specialist in all future pregnancies. I continued to be monitored when, later that night, the specialist came back to the hospital and told us that she was home and reviewing my file with ultrasounds and immediately came back to the hospital because of something she saw. I needed an emergency cesarean section. She suspected I had a placental abruption but could not be 100% sure until our baby was delivered.

As more doctors, nurses, anesthesiologists, nurse assistants, and more hospital staff than I could even imagine flooded into the room to prepare me, tears began rolling down my face. The specialist asked why I was crying and I said that I could not believe that it was happening again. She said no, this is different. Your baby is 27 weeks. Yes, he will need to remain in the hospital probably until his original due date. But at this point, he has a much better chance of surviving outside the womb than in. There was no purpose in delaying what may be inevitable--a c-section days later. It was highly probable that the placenta had detached from the uterine wall which would explain the dramatic reduction in amniotic fluid. An emergency c-section was critical.

I had to quickly wrap my mind around the idea. It would be okay. One of my brothers was premature and he is perfectly healthy. I knew plenty of people that were premature, and they had no issues. Our baby would be fine as well. He had been thriving this entire time. And like the specialist said, better out now than in. There were so many advances in technology that they could simulate the baby still being in the womb. He would be fine. Although still a bit nervous, I was calmer as they wheeled me into the surgery room.

A Time to Release

May 18, 2017. It was approximately 12:06am when the doctor pulled our baby from my womb. His scream and the life from his tiny little body was undeniable. Keven and I got to see him briefly before he was whisked away to the NICU. We were so happy. The doctors confirmed that I had indeed suffered a placental abruption. In fact, the placenta was nearly ready to pop out before our baby boy. Although not at all how we had expected or hoped, our baby boy was here.

I was high on drugs as they wheeled me to the recovery room. As I came to, I saw Keven and smiled. Our baby boy is here, and he is fine. The assistants then came to get Keven so he could see the baby. I was still a bit high and groggy, but so thankful. Then the doctor came to get me. I could not fully understand what she was saying in my still very groggy state, but I knew something was wrong. She asked me if I would like to see the baby and I said yes. They wheeled me to the NICU. The doctor said we have been trying to resuscitate him, would you like for us to keep going? I was still confused but I said yes. Then after what seemed like an eternity, the doctor turned to me and said he is gone. Their efforts had failed.

They had been attempting to resuscitate him for over an hour and it was not working. She then sent for Keven who had stepped outside into the hallway momentarily. She said we could see him and hold him. When she gave him to us, I looked down at our tiny baby in disbelief. He is not gone, he is fine. Just let me have him. Maybe he needs some skin to skin. The doctor said no, that will not help. They offered to clean him so we could hold him and say our goodbyes. We said no, he is fine. They allowed us to take him, tubes still hanging off him. We held him and talked to him and each other. Then we had to be transferred to our room.

In our room, we both held our baby boy and I prayed over him. I declared life over him. I said the doctors were wrong and he would show them. God would show them. He would perform a miracle and show His greatness. It would be a modern-day Lazarus healing. The miracle would be known throughout the hospital and beyond. People would recognize that Jesus is Lord and still performing miracles today. Keven could not bear it any longer and needed to go for some air. I was determined though. Our baby would live. I continued to pray over him. At this point, I had not shed a tear. I was in denial.

Then I called the nurse. I told her they could take him to clean him up but bring him right back to me. I continued to pray after they had taken him. Every time the door opened, I expected someone to run in and tell me that he was alive. They had him in the NICU but he was alive and doing fine. I could come see him. But, it never happened. They brought our baby back to me as I had insisted, and I continued to hold him and pray for resurrection. After some time, I felt defeat. I put him back in the baby bed and told the nurse that they could take him. He was going to the morgue.

Blue

We slept but later that morning, we insisted that the nurse bring our baby back. She warned us that after some hours in the morgue, he would not look the same. She tried to get us to reconsider. But, we were adamant. If you won't, then we will ask someone else who will. And we did. So, they brought our baby back to us. He was so tiny, barely over 1 lb. But, he still looked so cute. Not at all what you would expect death to look like. He was not eerily cold or pale. I held him and began speaking to him, again making declarations over his life. Maybe today God would perform the miracle we were so desperately seeking. Resurrection now would be an even greater miracle than had He performed it the day before. He did not come to raise Lazarus until he had been dead for 4 days, I rationalized.

As I continued to pray and speak to our baby, Keven once again became too overwhelmed and had to step out. I could tell that he wanted to stay but did not want to break in front of me. I watched him try to be strong for us both. Sometime after that, it finally hit me as I looked down at our baby boy. He was gone and he was not coming back. This was only his body.

Despite how perfect everything seemed up until I had to be admitted to the hospital, we had lost another one. And this one even more tragic and jarring than the last. I placed his body back into his bed and I wept. Where was God and How could He be so cruel to allow us to go through this again? And worse this time! Why give us hope just to have it snatched away so tragically and without notice?

I left our baby boy's body in his bed until after his grandparents were able to see it. First, Keven's mother came. Then, a couple of hours later, my parents arrived. They were each moved and expressed it in their own way. By that time, our baby boy's body had turned pale and it was obvious that there was no life left in it. After my parents saw him, I informed the nurse that she could take him. That was the last time I saw him until we received the little blue urn that matched his sister's of his cremated ashes.

Numb

This time was different and so much harder. We had to sign a birth certificate and a death certificate. Michael Angel is what we named him. Our second Angel. Yet, another funeral to plan.

Here I was, once again, recovering from childbirth, with no baby to show for it. Recovery from a cesarean section is much different than recovery from an induced vaginal birth. I was monitored much more closely and blood was drawn every four hours. Partly due to the second loss, my doctor wanted to find out if there was any other underlying issue that may be causing the losses. They tested me for everything.

Support from the hospital staff was incredible. Many of the same ones who assisted us with preparing for delivery and at delivery visited us to offer their condolences and even some others who had heard the news. All seemed just as shocked as we were and were baffled by his sudden passing. It did not make sense to them as it did not to us.

In the meantime, I developed a blood clot in my right leg so I had to begin receiving twice daily injections of Lovenox to prevent it from traveling to my lungs. I endured countless shots and blood tests over the course of the next week. I was referred to a hematologist for an even deeper inquiry into what may be occurring. I was drained.

A Time to Move

By the time I was discharged from the hospital over a week after having given birth to our Michael Angel and nearly three weeks after having been admitted, I had developed bruises from the innumerable shots that I had received. I had to be pricked in several places, some more than once, including my hands and in various places on my arms since my usual veins were depleted and scar tissue had formed reducing the ability to draw blood. I felt as if I was some sort of science experiment or pin cushion.

It was a solemn and somber drive home. My mother had flown back down to assist us as I recovered so she met us at the house. Keven had purchased a recliner for me so that I could be comfortable in the living room since it was advised that I not yet lay flat or climb up and down the stairs. Almost as soon as we got home and settled, we decided that we would need to move.

We could no longer live in this place, wherein we had begun preparations for not one but two babies and then lost both. I could not bear the idea of continuing to remain in this place that housed so much pain. Keven went to immediately inform the property manager that we would need to break our lease. We needed a fresh start.

Undone

    Later that evening, my chest began to hurt, and I experienced sharp pains as I attempted to take breaths. The doctors had advised me to immediately return to the hospital if I felt any pain in my chest as it could indicate that the blood clot had traveled to my lungs which can be fatal. However, I did not want to return to the hospital. Despite the possible outcome if the blood clot had indeed traveled to my lungs, I was adamant that I would not return to the hospital. It just felt like gas so if I can relieve the pressure from the gas, I would be fine. So, Keven purchased some GasX and ginger ale. Initially, they provided much needed relief and I was able to go to sleep. However, sometime in the night, the pain became more severe and I could only take short, belabored breaths to avoid the sharp pain. After trying to fight through it for a while, I woke up Keven and told him about the pain I was experiencing. He demanded that we go back to the hospital immediately.

    We went through the emergency room and explained what was going on, including that I had previously developed a blood clot and was currently on blood thinners. I was scheduled for a CT scan with contrast. Just as the doctor had informed us, the dye used to show contrast made me feel as if I was on fire briefly before going away just as suddenly. After the exam, we waited what seemed like hours for the results. Then, the doctor on duty, came to inform me that, good news, there was no blood clot in my lungs, but bad news, I had hospital-acquired pneumonia. Given my previous extended stay in the hospital, the doctor had mercy on me and stated that he would not keep me this time. He trusted me to take the antibiotics as prescribed and said that he would allow me to go home. After several hours, I was released to return home—with an active blood clot and now pneumonia on top of it. I felt so defeated but at the same time so relieved that I would not have to stay in the hospital any longer.

It seemed as if things went from worse to the worst within a short period of time. Later that day, after having received the pneumonia diagnosis, I tried to walk and could not. Because of the blood clot and the pneumonia, I had such unbearable pain in my leg and in my chest to the point that I could not straighten my back and could not fully lift my leg. Instead, I had to shuffle along tilted sideways and barely lifting my legs. I was so disheartened and felt so hopeless. I tried not to feel sorry for myself because things could be worse, right? But so what if they could be worse! They could also be so much better! It just is not fair that a child of God should have to endure so much. Where are you now God? You said you would never leave nor forsake us. But guess what, I feel completely abandoned and forsaken. I had no words for God and hardly any for anyone else. All I could do was cry.

This time, counseling could not help. What could a counselor possibly say to me to encourage me—that it would not happen again? Too late, it did. Even after I believed and put my complete hope and trust in the Lord declaring His word over Michael Angel even more than what we did for Angel Taylor. Nothing a counselor would say could allow me to trust like that again. Because, frankly, you do not know. And despite God in all His mercy and love, He just did not come through for us this time. I am angry, I am sad, I am hopeless, and I do not care about anything anymore.

A Time to Chill

For the next several weeks, I mainly stayed in the living room and binged shows and movies on Netflix. I barely spoke to anyone unless they came to the house. I did a little bit of legal work because after all, despite your own personal tragedy, clients have needs. Most were understanding while others seemed like they almost expected us to take a week or two but then get back to tending to their "emergencies" and every need. I was just so tired of it all. I was barely sleeping so I was tired all of the time.

We were barely maintaining as Keven obviously felt the weight of this loss heavier than Angel just as I did. This time, it took a few weeks for my milk to come in. But once again, I was staring in the mirror, dripping milk and my completely flattened stomach and could not help but scream or cry every time I saw it. After awhile, I just stopped looking in the mirror.

After Angels

Guilt

After two losses and despite what anyone may say in an effort to comfort, a barrage of questions haunted me. Was Angel Taylor miserable? Why did she not move much even after prompting and prodding? Even though I was having a pain crisis, maybe I should not have taken any medication with Michael Angel. Did the medication harm our baby, despite the doctor's assurances? Did our babies have pain? What could I have possibly done differently? I tried to eat healthily and follow proper nutrition for Angel Taylor and we lost her. I tried not to be as hardcore about it with Michael Angel—still getting a proper nutrition but I treated myself more to those things that I liked but may not have been the most nutritional. And we lost him. I am at my wit's end.

I cannot help but to feel guilty, as though I had a part in killing our babies. Does Keven blame me? Does he wish that he had married someone else and they would already have their beautiful babies without any effort? Maybe he wants to leave so as to not allow himself to get hurt anymore. Maybe he does not want to take care of me anymore as so much of these past couple of years, I have been the cause of so much of his grief. So many unanswered questions and I hate myself/my body for causing all of this.

Night

After several weeks of being unable to sleep, I asked Keven to get me some sleeping pills. I had always been one to avoid taking any sort of pills or medicines as I preferred to handle sickness naturally, but this time I did not care. I was already taking blood thinning pills after all. Despite my abandoning my natural healing techniques, I did not want to immediately reach out to my doctor for a prescription as she had offered. Instead, I wanted something non-habit forming and non-drowsy. Something that would just help me sleep. He got me ZZZQuil. It was not that strong, but it seemed to help in the beginning.

Once I finished the first box, I asked Keven to purchase some more. While he was out getting the pills and other things, I imagined that maybe I could take enough where I would no longer wake up. Where I could sleep forever. Then I would not have to endure this pain and hopelessness any longer. I imagined what life would be like without me here. My family and friends will be fine, I thought. They may be sad and upset initially, but they will manage and be alright. They would understand.

But then I thought about how Keven would manage. Would he be better off without me? I looked around our new place, at all our things, at our furniture, Keven's paintings, our photos and travel souvenirs, at the life we had built together, that we were building together. I could not bear the thought of the heartache he would experience by losing me too. He had already endured so much. It would not be fair to make him go through that. I had to endure. We could get through this together. We made our vows, through sickness and in health. Despite my own despair, I could not bear the idea of being the cause of any additional heartache or sorrow to my husband. Yes, I had and am enduring so much. But so is he. No way I can add to that. He still loved me despite our losses. That had not changed. He had already shown me that. So, I must keep pushing.

Keven came home and stated that he did not feel comfortable with getting me any more sleeping pills, that I needed to find other ways to manage, so he did not buy them. He was my saving grace in more ways than one and he had no idea.

A Time to Be

Our anniversary came, the day our baby boy was due, and I was so depressed. I did not want to talk to anyone. All around me, people were pregnant and happy or had just had their healthy little ones, including some very close and dear to me. But, I could not fully celebrate in their joy when I was suffering from so much misery and the thought of having lost two in a row. I would see or hear about people who did not even want children giving birth to beautiful, healthy babies. Or those who did not take care of their bodies, such as drinking, smoking, or other harmful things even while pregnant, yet still giving birth to beautiful, healthy babies. Life just was not fair.

Not that I was perfect or lived the perfect life. But, why did I lose these two dear babies when I did everything in my power to ensure their health? It was my lifestyle to guard my eyes and ears so that my spirit was as pure as possible. I did not curse, I did not drink alcohol, I did not smoke, I never had multiple sexual partners, only my husband, I did not listen to vile music or watch vile shows, I did everything that I could to protect myself physically and spiritually. Yet, despite all of this, my body caused my husband and me to lose two babies. What did living this lifestyle matter anymore?

I might as well eat and drink whatever I want, live how I want to live, watch what I want to watch, live recklessly without a care. Who cares about what God thinks? Obviously, it did not matter anyways because it did not make a difference. I found it extremely difficult to pray so I did not pray. I could barely say a grace for my food. I did not think God was listening. He was not listening when I begged and pleaded for Him to bring our daughter back and He did not listen when I begged and pleaded for Him to bring our son back. Despite our declarations and prayers, we lost them both. So why pray now? For what? He was not listening anyways. All I wanted to do was scream and shout and cry and curse and break things. But, I mostly suffered in silence.

I did not want to burden my husband with my despair and anguish because he was trying to manage and deal with his own. No counselor could help. And I did not want to speak with any family or friends because none of them had been through anything similar. No one I knew had experienced anything like what I had experienced. Although I knew some who had suffered miscarriages in early pregnancy and could understand the pain of loss, I did not think that any of them could fully understand my pain and torment because of the additional layers of trauma from delivery and burial of our babies. I chose to remain silent and drown out my thoughts. Instead, I kept a smile on my face and pretended as if everything was fine. I did not talk about it and nobody seemed to notice. Things were back to normal. It was something sad that happened and we had moved on just like everyone else.

But internally, I was still screaming and wrestling with my emotions. I had so many moments of ups and downs, but primarily downs. I still was not sleeping well. Keven fell into painting after we lost Angel Taylor. That was his outlet. But, I could not figure out mine. I wanted to dance or do something active, but I was still recovering. I tried to drown myself in my work, but it did nothing but to distract me for a few moments at a time.

Then, I decided, what if we just give it all up. We need some time to recalibrate and to just be. I approached Keven with the idea of winding down the firm and traveling. He always knew me to have a travel bug and wanderlust spirit since we met. I had even suggested that we take some time to live and work abroad for a couple of years prior to having children. But, the timing was never right. We were building the firm and trying to get some things in order here in the States. But now, he was open to the idea. We were both mentally and physically exhausted. This was the perfect time to just go and be free.

This excited me, and I began to pour myself into researching opportunities abroad as well as attempting to map out our travels. My excitement must have been contagious because Keven became involved in exploring our travel options, which he had always left up to me. The very idea provided me with renewed purpose and motivation to keep going. It helped to ease my anxiety and depression. I stopped wallowing in sorrow but began experiencing joy again.

Red

October 6, 2017. One year after I gave birth to Angel. I was looking forward to receiving good news. I was excited about our upcoming travel plans and physically, I was feeling much better. It was the day of my checkup to see if I could stop taking the blood thinners. Keven and I were optimistic. The hematologist was optimistic as well as he had reviewed my previous blood test results from June and noted that my levels were normal, great in fact. I had not taken any of the blood thinner medication in a couple of weeks and the doctor was hopeful that I would not have to as we moved forward. Several blood tests were ordered then Keven and I left the appointment in good spirits. Things were finally beginning to turn around for us.

However, that weekend, I began experiencing an indescribable feeling in my right leg. It was not painful, but it felt funny, similar to how it had felt when the initial blood clot was first discovered. On Monday, I called the hematologist to advise him of what I was feeling, and he ordered an ultrasound of my leg, especially since my coagulation levels were elevated per the most recent blood work.

The appointment confirmed my suspicion. I had a blood clot. Now, to determine whether it was the same clot that had not fully resolved or a new clot. If it was the same clot, it would indicate that I would need to stay on the blood thinners to prevent any further clotting. If it was a new one, that would not be good news, according to the doctor, because it could be an indicator of something more serious.

    The results indicated that it was a new clot. This time in a major vein which made it more dangerous. My primary care physician referred me to a cardiothoracic surgeon since now I had a history of blood clots and it may be necessary to implant a filter to prevent the clot from traveling to my lungs. Here we go again. As if I had not already suffered enough. Now I possibly needed surgery and it was dangerous to climb stairs (we lived on the third floor).

    My leg began hurting again to the point that I could not put any pressure on it. If Keven was not home, I had to stay indoors as it was unsafe for me to try to ascend and descend the stairs on my own. This was not feasible to continue long-term, so we would have to move yet again. The joy that I thought I had as we were planning our travels quickly vanished.

Flawed

I am so unhappy. Every time that things seem to be improving, it is as if something worse happens to bring us back down to our miserable reality. We are still working to wind down the firm because even if we cannot begin our travels as we would like, we need a break from this responsibility. We return to the doctor to review the results of my last bloodwork. I am waiting with bated breath as he goes over the results. I had already reviewed many of them on MyChart and discussed them with my mom. But, I waited to hear his explanation of some of the results.

They determined the cause of our losses. It was called protein S deficiency, an issue where the body lacks enough anti-coagulation factors, so it is predisposed to creating blood clots, something that is only discovered in most people when it is too late—after they have experienced a number of losses. The doctor was certain that small blood clots had formed behind the placenta during both pregnancies essentially killing some portions of the placenta thus limiting nutrients given to the baby and causing intra-uterine growth restriction.

Most women have early term miscarriages with protein S deficiency, so the hematologist marveled at the fact that my pregnancies lasted through 24-27 weeks. Though a point of intended encouragement, it seems all the more difficult that the pregnancies did go through so many weeks—after we had gotten attached to the idea of our babies, seen them move and grow, after feeling Michael kick and move and respond to our voices for a number of weeks and then so suddenly lose them both. Although loss is difficult regardless of the stage, would it have been easier to endure and to accept had it happened earlier on as "most women" with this deficiency? Either way, I wish this experience on no woman.

After leaving the doctor's office, I began to feel slightly encouraged. Keven was in much better spirits given that we finally have an answer—some medical explanation for the losses. The doctors are not saying that we should not attempt to have children but that there is hope. It is an "easy fix" and with treatment, we can have healthy babies. I try to convince myself that everything is fine, to share his optimism, and it will only get better as time progresses. Yes, I will have to inject myself twice a day with heparin shots. But, it will all be worth it when we are holding our healthy, full term, beautiful baby.

I would be lying if I did not admit that I am still fearful and not so optimistic. Of course, I do my research and encounter many success stories so that restores some optimism. But, I am still upset and saddened. Why did God not think enough of us to prevent this from ever happening in the first place? Though I would love to trust and depend on Him in future pregnancies and not rely on doctors and medication, I do not have the capability, willpower, or bravery to do that anymore. I trusted Him to save my babies and look where we are. No way I can even attempt to go through another pregnancy without following the advice of the doctors.

As much as I hate the idea of it, I guess I will be injecting myself twice daily in future pregnancies. If I decide to attempt to carry in the future. I have always dreamt of carrying my own children. But given the two losses, no way we can endure another. My heart just cannot take anymore. Either way, children are far in the future now. I need time to recover physically and we both need time to recover mentally and emotionally.

A Time to Travel

    The truly great news that came from my appointment is that our travels could move forward as planned. The first ten days of a clot being formed is the most dangerous as it is more likely to break off and travel in those days. My hematologist insisted that I would have no issues so long as I remained on the blood thinners. Unfortunately, I would have to remain on the blood thinners indefinitely. But finally, some good news for real. We can recalibrate, recover and live life free for a bit. I allowed the excitement to creep back in and I was in much better spirits as we continued seeking and mapping out options for our great adventure.

    Due to Hurricane Irma in South Florida, we were unable to wind down the firm when we would have liked as court dates were pushed back to accommodate the weeks that the courts and judicial system were closed. Thus, we decided to do part of our trip prior to a trial that Keven had at the end of the year and then we would map out the rest of our journey after the holidays. For the first time, I felt that there may be an avenue to joy after the losses. Because my dream had always been to travel the world, mostly for humanitarian reasons, but nonetheless, travel, I thought maybe our losses will provide the motivation we need to begin our worldwide journey. Not that we could not travel with children, but not having children provided much more flexibility and was far cheaper. I finally felt that I was back on track to purpose and destiny. We can live life free, without encumbrance or hindrance.

Maybe we could do this for two to three years and then revisit having children after we have traveled the world as a couple. I found comfort in the thought that through our hurt and pain that God was propelling us into the place we were truly intended to be.

Green

We lived as we traveled through several countries, eating various foods, experiencing new cultures, and learning more about ourselves and each other in the process. Keven is my best travel partner as we both have very adventurous spirits and enjoy trying new things, whether it be food or experiences.

Keven's energy was infectious as random strangers would often join us in dancing or speaking in our videos. I learned to become more comfortable in front of the camera as he continuously put me on the spot while filming our adventures. We lived carefree as we immersed ourselves in the history of some countries while allowing the waves to crash all around us on the beaches of others.

Although we knew almost no one on our excursions, we lived, laughed and enjoyed an inexplicable bond with those who were once strangers. It was perfect, and I could not wait to begin part two of our travels. If I could give everything up now and continue our adventure, there would be absolutely no hesitation. Take everything, Lord, and just let this be life. I knew that all was well in the world and this was my new destiny.

Although I could still feel the pain of the losses, it was no longer as deep. A crazy way to get one's attention but maybe just maybe God was trying to get me to accomplish those things I had pushed aside. Those things that were deep within my heart from as early as I can remember.

I had finally found consolation despite our losses and I felt as if I was able to deal with my emotions and thoughts. I was finally happy again. We were not ready to return to the States, but we had to. There are so many things that we have to do that prevent us from continuing our travels at this time. But I anxiously anticipate our return to traveling even as we fly back home.

Dark

We got back to the States and all the emotions that I had bottled up over the past several months, and especially during our time of traveling, came flooding back. Despite all of my efforts, I had to acknowledge and accept that I was not okay. I broke down and thought if I just get my thoughts out into a letter, I might feel better. And I did. But, just like everything else before, it only allowed a temporary reprieve from my pain and heartache.

I knew that the devil wanted me to hold onto the pain and hurt in my heart and blame God. Although I knew, I just could not break free but instead was an active participant in allowing the negative thoughts to control my mind. I was angry at God and though I know He is a just God that I could trust, I could not move past the pain because I felt so betrayed. Although it hurt, I could manage the loss of our baby girl. We had an idea that everything might not be okay with her from almost the beginning.

However, God could have saved our son, but He did not. Why would He allow us to even bring our baby boy into this world, with all the signs of life, health and vitality, just to have him snatched away from us so suddenly? Despite us doing everything expected as God-fearing Christians! This was unforgivable. I just wanted to give up on God.

At the beginning of my pregnancy with Angel, I was the closest to God as I had ever been. I was truly seeking Him daily and in everything that I did. So, it was a huge blow when we lost her. But, as I was finding my way back to Him, determined that I could not give up, that He never fails, that He never leaves nor forsakes His children, that He is a sovereign God perfect in all of His ways, we lost Michael. And now I have a scar to constantly remind me of this loss. I cannot help but replay it in my mind. The events leading up to the c-section, the c-section itself and how our world came crashing down once again just a few hours after delivering our baby boy. How could I ever get past this? How could I ever truly trust again? How could I ever let my guard down again? I truly did not know how. As much as I searched my heart and soul and tried to remind myself of God's grace and mercy, I was still so angry and hurt and full of resentment.

My doctor diagnosed me with a mood disorder and referred me to a behavioral health specialist. I thought maybe it would be beneficial to seek counseling once again. Nothing else has been helping, after all. Maybe I need to just talk with someone to get my thoughts out there. Even if I do not find their advice to be that helpful, maybe a sounding board is what I need. Someone to just listen to me vent without me feeling as if I am burdening them and putting a strain on our relationship. Although I knew I could share with Keven, my emotions were so heavy. He was grieving as well so I felt it might even be counterproductive to his own recovery.

Reality is that the bliss of travel was fleeting. No more sipping the world's greatest hot chocolate after having floated through the icy waterways of Venice in a romantic gondola ride. No more sitting on the shores of Paphos taking in the beauty of God's creation while Keven dives underneath the waters. No more wandering the streets of Barcelona taking in the grandeur of the contrasting modern and gothic architecture.

Reality is that Angel is gone. Reality is that Michael is gone. Reality is that I am sinking rapidly into an abyss of darkness. I accepted the referral to the behavioral health specialist. It was time to deal with this reality.

A Time to Watch

I had not been to church in several months, maybe once or twice in the entire year. This was unusual but had become our new normal. I did not want the attention from the members at our usual church and I could not bear entertaining questions about the baby - again. I was not ready to face them, to provide explanation, to receive sympathy, to be fake. I was not interested in pretending that all was well in my world despite my circumstances. I was not ok. I did not feel like pretending that I was full of the joy of the Lord. I did not even feel like pretending that I was happy. I was still so deeply wounded and did not feel the least bit blessed. I did not feel special or noticed by God. I did not think He was listening to my heart anymore. I did not think He cared all that much. Though, I knew the members always meant well, I just was not ready and did not have the strength to put up a façade. So, I stayed away.

I also was not comfortable going to other churches because I still was not able to pray and much less worship and reverence God. It would just be an awkward experience that I rather not put myself through. How do I worship the God who would not and did not respond in my time of need, even when I believed, even when I begged, even when I pleaded? I felt as if I had been ignored and pushed to the side. After having been in such a pit of despair for so long without any reprieve or acknowledgment from God, it was hard to imagine going somewhere to worship that same God. If God needed me or even wanted me, He knew where to find me. To respond. To let me know

He is listening. He had always known how to get my attention in the past, so He can still just as easily get my attention now. I simply did not feel like faking it. So, I stayed away.

Keven, however, was finding his way back to God much quicker and easier than me. He would begin to release little seeds of faith occasionally. *"I believe God sees exactly where we are." "God is doing something great in our lives." "I am thankful that God gave us each other for such a tough season."* He began reintroducing God in a way that was subtle yet sure. He was fighting his way through his own pain yet his desire for a relationship with God began to bubble up again. I watched him. I listened. In the depths of my spirit, I knew he meant well, but we were not on the same page. I was still so jaded.

Although we did not have plans for New Year's Eve except spend some time with family, Keven felt led for us to go to his cousin's church. The leading to go to church was so abrupt. We were in the car, dressed down in casual clothes, driving in the opposite direction from the church and about a mile from his sister's home when he mentioned going to watchnight service. We had had no intentions to be in anybody's service that night. The plan was for us to play with our beautiful nieces and perhaps experience some fireworks with them by our side, if any of us managed to stay awake.

We had been to his cousin's church before though, years ago. The pastor and first lady are apostles and God used them to speak prophetically to us in prior visits. Although I was not completely for the idea of going to church and worshiping God, I was not completely opposed to it either, surprisingly. I thought maybe they would have a word for us. Besides, nothing else that I was doing (i.e. trying to distract myself or ignore how I felt) or not doing (i.e. praying and going to church) was helping my situation get any better. I had taken the behavioral therapist referral from my doctor but had yet to complete my intake. There was nothing to lose so we went.

Initially, just as I had suspected, it was awkward. We sat near the front as the ushers had directed us. It was near impossible to just sit down and spectate. People expected us to get up and worship along with them—to sing celebratory songs of God's greatness. So, I stood as I felt mandated. I might have lifted my hands in feigned reverence. I did not feel anything in my heart but pain and my thoughts began to drift. I imagined being anywhere but at that service. I felt as if I should have stuck with my first inclination and just stayed away as opposed to faking it and feeling compelled to do something that I was not all that interested in doing.

Some of the songs spoke to my heart and I began to feel something familiar. But, I did not want to give in to it. I did not want to get on an emotional high from the music and dancing just to be let down once again after leaving the presence of the service. I refused to be betrayed again – by hope, by faith, by God.

A Time to Rebuild

I continued on in this battle in my mind as the Watchnight Service progressed. Should I let the worship overtake me or should I continue to guard my heart? Then, it was time for the message.

There was a guest preacher for the New Year's Eve (watchnight) service. We felt as if everything he had to say was geared directly towards us. That the leading Keven felt that night was intentional as God scripted a message specifically tailored to where we were. *"We can be so much more if we allowed God to heal us from tragic memories. We are powerful and are not limited by our tribulations. We are more than what we have experienced. God still has a plan for our lives if we can just push past the trauma."*

It seemed as if right as I was ready to give up, to either sleep forever or just merely exist, God spoke to my husband's heart to have us drive to a specific church and hear a specific message strategically designed to penetrate our pain and paralysis. It appeared God led us to that service to firmly tell us enough was enough. He let us wallow in our misery when it was a time to mourn. He let us abandon our goals and aspirations when it was a time to heal. And now it was a time to build.

It was time to rebuild our foundation in God, to fortify our spiritual walls, to restore purpose and reclaim identity. My temple was desolate, barren and ugly and it was time to restore. It was time to build. We had been stagnant for too long. But now, it was time to align with the vision of progress. Something began to stir within me.

We were derailed as we were dealt a powerful blow and our vision was distorted to the extent that it seemed near impossible to find our way back. But it was time. I saw the pathway beginning to light before me once again. We have work to do. We have the capacity for greatness. We will not be defeated. Despite the reality of our painful past, we are still flowing with electric potential. We were made in God's image and have the power to speak light into darkness, to create. We can speak light into the darkness that had made its way into our hearts and minds. We can speak freedom from depression and despair. With God's love flowing through us, we can rebuild.

Despite the initial awkwardness and my resistance, I left the New Year's Eve service feeling so rejuvenated and ready to conquer the world. After months of being unplugged, I felt the dynamic energy of becoming re-plugged into the most powerful source of all. God, our Father and Creator. I was charged. Though it was not a scripture that was mentioned at the NYE service, I kept repeating *"Work out your salvation with fear and trembling; for it is God who is at work in you, both to will and to work for His good pleasure."* (Philippians 2:12b-13, NASB) For some reason, this scripture truly resonated with me. I was tired of being miserable and ready to let God work in me again for His good pleasure—whatever that is.

God Is

God Is My Comfort

All of the pain I had lugged around after the loss of my Angels did not miraculously dissolve when the clock struck twelve during that New Year's Eve watchnight service. The consciousness that I was in a new year did not radically shift my thinking or free me from all shame and guilt. The beautiful fireworks, the dancing and singing did not make me feel any less ugly. But in that service, God performed a miracle. It was as if He physically touched my heart and warmth began to emanate from it. Something changed within me that night and this time it was not the power of a child of purpose growing within me. This time it was love – God's love chipping away at my stony heart.

That night, my heart once again became vulnerable to God and His word. I could remember Him and His love towards me. I began to remember the things He has done for me. I remembered that He had designated a plan for my life. I remembered that He had always led me on that path of destiny. That night, I was free to consider God. I felt power growing within me, quickly and rapidly. I was not weak. I was powerful. I was not ugly. I was beautiful. I was not defeated. I was more than a conqueror. I began to feel as if I could really conquer this thing with God's grace. The revelation was instantaneous. I *could* allow Him to heal my heart. I *could* acknowledge God's capacity. I *could* recognize His greatness despite my circumstances. I *could* trust Him, again.

That night, I received the conviction to truly remember God. Not just who God is *to me*, but who

God is. I was guilty of minimizing the greatness of God by viewing Him through the lens of my limited human experiences and the variances of their shades. I saw Him through pain and He was merciless. I saw Him through grief and He was distant.

I had gone so long being bitter and angry and disappointed with God that although I could finally acknowledge who He had been to me, I also needed to acknowledge the power, grace and love of God in my life in my present situation. I could not see my blessing nor feel the rain of His favor in my life while being consumed with trauma and suffering. I needed a reminder.

Several days after the New Year's Eve service, the book of Job continued to resound in my spirit. Initially, I ignored it because although I knew that I had been living a righteous life, I would never compare myself to Job. I would think of his story often but never did I consider myself worthy enough for God to test me in that manner. I did not "curse God and die" through my own tribulation, but I sure did not remain as upright and holy as Job had been throughout his season of trauma. So, I continued to dismiss the urge to read about Job.

However, after numerous times of the thought coming to mind (the Holy Spirit nudging me), I picked up my Bible to read. I immediately flipped to Job 38 per the nudging, where God begins His response to Job's questioning. Although Job had the grace to bless God during his season of trauma, acknowledging that God has the capacity to give and take away, he still had some pointed questions for God. Job asked, "*Why did*

I not die at birth, come out of the womb and expire?" (Job 3:11, NASB). Job began to imagine that a quick and early death would be preferable than living in abundance only to suffer such a terrible plight. An early death would free him from the torment of reality. He would have no children to suffer early and tragic deaths. There would be no scar to heal, no tears to dry, no void to fill. Job's question spoke to me. Maybe it was better to have suffered a quick and early death than to have to endure such heartache.

Throughout the book of Job, Job's friends accused him of wrongdoing and being the cause of his own sorrow and losses. Job maintained his innocence and even tried to convince God of the same. After extended silence by God, God responded to Job in such a powerful way:

> *Where were you when I laid the foundations of the earth? Tell Me, if you have understanding, Who set its measurements? Since you know. Or who stretched the line on it?...Have you ever in your life commanded the morning, And caused the dawn to know its place,...*
> Job 38:4-12 (NASB)

As I began reading, I thought "well Lord, you are getting right to the point I see." Despite having distanced myself from God, I was still able to hear Him say that He was not rebuking me but sent me to these scriptures to remind me of His glory and power. I read and meditated on the scriptures. God asks Job a series of questions while declaring His own majesty, the marvelousness of His works.

Though I had read these scriptures many times in the past, this was the first time I truly dwelt and meditated on what God was saying. The imagery of His majesty commanded my attention. God is truly powerful beyond measure. The very God who defined the measurements of the earth and all that is within it knows who I am. This same God, who laid the foundations of the earth and commands the sun to rise each day, created me and gave me a purpose. I heard God. And then, after having declared His own magnificence to Job and describing who He is, God restored all that Job lost plus so much more. He was the God who restored.

In addition to leading me to specific scriptures to read for enlightenment and empowerment, God began flooding my life with comfort and reassurances. God sent messengers to encourage me and confirm some things that He shared with me in private. Some of these messengers were complete strangers who had no way of knowing what God shared with me in secret, but God was clearly on a mission to get my attention. And He did.

> *Blessed be the God and Father of our Lord Jesus Christ, the Father of mercies and God of all comfort, who comforts us in all our tribulation, that we may be able to comfort those who may be in trouble, with the comfort which we ourselves are comforted by God.* 2 Corinthians 1:3-4 (NKJV)

When I began to realize that *God will comfort us in all our tribulation* did not read *God will keep us from all tribulation*, my perspective began to shift. It was a profound revelation that I had forgotten. In life, there are some challenges that we will simply have to endure. Our tribulations, and the waves and depths of pain in which they bring, do not minimize God's capacity for greatness or His love towards us. God did not promise that we will not face hardship. He did promise, however, to comfort us when we go through our tribulation and to never leave nor forsake us.

The scripture also says that God comforts us that we may be able to comfort those who may be in trouble. How can we truly sympathize with the suffering of others if God rescues us from all our tribulations when we ask? How do we connect with the degree of pain our peers may experience if we cannot identify with their trauma? How do I know God as a comforter if I have nothing to be comforted from? I began to hear God.

God is the comforter of our souls. Even when the pain seems as if it reaches the depths of your soul, He will send His Holy Spirit to whisper to your heart or to your conscience, to bring comfort. Even when the pain seemed as if it threatened to swallow me, God showed up with revelation of His desire to restore me and comfort me in my time of tribulation. Whether it be directly through the Holy Spirit or the Holy Spirit working through a man or woman of God, He will comfort. Just as Jesus informs us in John 14:26,

> *But the Comforter, which is the Holy Ghost, whom the Father will send in my name, he shall teach you all things, and bring all things to your remembrance, whatsoever I have said unto you.* (KJV)

God will remind you of the things that He has pronounced over you. Those things that He proclaimed long ago. Even if you have forgotten in your misery, He will bring it back to your remembrance. Just as He reminded me of His brilliance, of His splendor, of His comfort, He can do the same for you if you let Him.

God Is My Strength

After peeling back the hardened layers of my heart and leading me on a journey of remembrance, of God as my comforter, the Holy Spirit encouraged me to read Isaiah 40 (NASB)—another scripture that I had read often in the past, one of my favorite passages as a matter of fact. Isaiah 40:12-14 completely drew me in:

> *Who has measured the waters in the hollow of His hand, and marked off the heavens by the span, and calculated the dust of the earth by the measure, and weighed the mountains in a balance and the hills in a pair of scales? Who has directed the Spirit of the Lord, or as His counselor has informed Him? With whom did He consult and who gave Him understanding? And who taught Him in the path of justice and taught Him knowledge and informed Him of the way of understanding?*

The scripture resonated with my spirit. God is so magnificent and wise, how can man even understand the depth of His acts? It is impossible except that which God reveals to us. For the first time in a long time, I was able to take my eyes off my loss, my trauma, my body and gaze upon the greatness of God and marvel. He transcends my circumstances. He is magnified above my tribulations. He is exalted beyond my perspective. He is God Almighty. After describing His sheer majesty, He leaves us with a promise that:

> *...those who wait upon the Lord will gain new strength, they will mount up with wings like eagles, they will run*

and not get tired, they will walk and not become weary. v. 31.

After losing our Angels, I was beyond weary. I was full of despair but refused to seek God for strength and endurance. But in addition to providing comfort, God reminded me that He has the capacity and desire to strengthen me, if I would only let Him. I was discouraged, depressed, and ready to give up, but I could gain renewed strength, if I receive it. I could mount up and soar above my circumstances like an eagle. God gives strength to the weary, but for such a long time, I was not ready to acknowledge God in the midst of my trials. But God can be the God of our fiery furnace if we let Him.

God promises to restore and give us strength. In fact, He loves us so much He encourages us to *"cast all your anxiety/burdens on Him."* (1 Peter 5:7, NASB). We can be free from agony if we would only recognize that God is willing to bear it for us. I am guilty of dismissing God and His love. Though it was hard for me to feel His presence many times throughout my pain and suffering, He never left me. He gives us so many promises in His Word of the same. He tells us frankly that He *"directs the steps of the godly. He delights in every detail of their lives. Though they stumble, they will never fall, for the Lord holds them by the hand."* Psalm 37:23-24 (NLT, emphasis added). Although I stumbled into my pit of despair and wallowed in the depth of my sorrow, God was there, and He saw me. He carried me and cared for me. He kept me.

Just as God kept me even as I fell further and deeper into my anguish, He can keep you. He still holds your hand. He will not let it go or let you fall. It does not matter what your unique circumstances are. You may stumble but you can rise again. It may seem as if you are losing, but you will not be destroyed. You will live. You can survive. Despite any apprehension that you may have in allowing God to mend what you think is broken and irreparable, He can. And He will, if you let Him.

> *...that He would grant you, according to the riches of His glory, <u>to be strengthened with power through His Spirit</u> in the inner man, so that Christ may dwell in your hearts through faith; and that you, being rooted and grounded in love, may be able to comprehend with all the saints what is the breadth and length and height and depth, and to know the love of Christ which surpasses knowledge, that you may be filled up to all the fullness of God.* (Ephesians 3:16-19, NASB, emphasis added)

The love of Christ surpasses our knowledge. It may be difficult for us to grasp immediately after losing a child, while being consumed with grief, while feeling ashamed. Sometimes we expect God to see us how we see ourselves. But God's love is perfect and pure. As God melted the icy layers of my heart, as He poured in and warmed it up with His love, as He comforted my bruised heart, He became the God who strengthened me through His Spirit. He can do the same for you, if you let Him.

God Is My Creator

The Holy Spirit took me on a journey of reading the Word and inclining my thoughts to who God is. I had become so overwhelmed with my circumstances that I could not see or sense Him anymore. I had read many scriptures about who God is, scriptures that describe in great detail the immense splendor of God. I read about God my comforter and God my strength, when the Holy Spirit brought me to Psalm 139. It was time to rediscover God as my creator.

Navigating through Psalm 139 was bittersweet as this passage speaks of God's understanding and thoughts towards us as our Creator. In a season in which my self-concept had waned, it was refreshing to meditate on the God who knows me and values me. But, this scripture was not foreign to us. We had read Psalm 139:13-17 (NIV) almost daily to our son, Michael Angel. After losing Angel Taylor, I felt it necessary to speak this declaration over all our children, to let them know who they are even while in the womb while also reminding God of who He is as our Creator.

For you created my inmost being;
you knit me together in my mother's womb.
I praise you because I am fearfully and wonderfully made;
your works are wonderful,
I know that full well.
My frame was not hidden from you
when I was made in the secret place,

> *when I was woven together in the depths of the earth.*
> *Your eyes saw my unformed body;*
> *all the days ordained for me were written in your book*
> *before one of them came to be.*
> *How precious to me are your thoughts,*
> *Or How amazing are your thoughts concerning me God!*
> *How vast is the sum of them!*

The scripture was a daily declaration. Reading this passage encouraged me while also making me somewhat sorrowful. I was encouraged that God knew me so well and had my days written in His book. But deeply saddened that the only days that were written for Angel Taylor and Michael Angel were the short months that they spent in my womb. For whatever the reason, it was ordained that I would carry them each only for a short period of time before they would have to leave us. It was difficult to digest.

I began to meditate on the revelation regarding the scriptures. Although I felt worthless, God knit me together in my mother's womb with a strategic design and plan. Although I felt ugly, God made me so wonderfully complex. I was fearfully and wonderfully made. God created my inmost being. My heart, my mind, my spirit, my body were created by God with intention. I am not worthless. I am not ugly. I am wonderfully made.

While allowing the Holy Spirit to rebuild my self-concept and restore the revelation of God my Creator, the sadness in my heart after losing my Angels remained. I could not help considering that my babies were snatched from me before God had completed knitting them together in my womb. While they were being made in the secret place, their fearfully and wonderfully made lives ceased to be before completion.

It was a tough pill to swallow and painful to contemplate. But, after the several weeks prior of reading about and meditating on who God is, I was able to overcome and not allow my thoughts to sink me into a place of despair and darkness again. Instead, I allowed this confirmation of His thoughts towards us to lift me up.

I began to trust my Creator again. Even though my vision of myself and my perspective of God is still a bit distorted, I have begun to trust Him and His Word again. God knows me. He knows me better than I know myself. He is my Creator. God knows Angel Taylor. He knows Michael Angel. His eyes saw our unframed bodies. Our frames were not hidden from Him. Our days have been measured by Him. I began to receive His Word and His plan. Despite our losses and what I still often feel about my body, I am still a work of art crafted by the skillful and masterful hands of our Creator. As will be our children.

God has purposed each and every one of us on this earth for a time and a season. He has not only counted the days of our lives but ordained each one. He wrote every single one of our days even before we were born. We are here with purpose, for purpose and on purpose. God is our creator.

Despite if you believe your body has failed you and is the source of your shame. Despite if you believe you are ugly and worthless. Despite if you believe that nothing good is left in your body and all virtue has been depleted. God has made you so wonderfully complex. You may bend but you will not break. You may stumble, but He will not let you fall. He will allow you to withstand the flames of your fiery furnace. You are a work of art fashioned by the Ultimate Creator and the One who knows you will lift you up, if you let Him.

A Time to Dance

I still have triggers and moments of apprehension. But, the callous that was forming around my heart was stripped away. And I can honestly say, only God could have done that. Once I allowed Him back in, He proved to me once again who He truly is. There is no reason to have trust issues with Him. He still is and always will be perfect in all of His ways.

I may not ever fully understand why He allowed us to lose our babies. But, I do know that God is sovereign and righteous and loves us so much. Although I am still not yet ready to try again to have any children, I know that when the time comes, I will be ready and I will fully trust Him once again. He has already given Keven and me visions of our children. He has sent His prophets to confirm the same. We have hope and we know that they will come. For whatever the reason, it just was not time yet.

If you are ever in a place where you do not know who you are or who God called you to be, He can remind you if you let Him. If you are ever blinded by the fog of your tribulations, by the aching pain of your trauma, and cannot find conviction to dance, God can heal your heart and restore your sight. God who spoke you into existence knows exactly who you are, your capacity, your purpose. He knows His plan for your life.

You are great. You are powerful. You are filled with endless potential. You are more than the limitations placed on you by man or society. You are more than the limitations placed on you by your own thinking or perception. Your beauty transcends aesthetics captured by an eye. It encompasses the curves of your mind, the fullness of your understanding, the freedom of your soul and the strength of your spirit. No matter how many pieces of yourself that you feel you have lost, God can mend those pieces and restore the vision of who you are to yourself. You can see yourself as valuable again. You can see yourself as powerful again.

Just as God can remind you of who you are and restore your value, He can remind you of who He is. He is wonderful. He is marvelous. He is full of splendor. He knows the depths of our being. He is majestic. He is Lord. He is Creator. He is the God of your soul. He is the God of your spirit. He is the God of your body. He still longs for a relationship with you despite how far you may distance yourself from Him. The depth of His wisdom and knowledge and understanding is beyond our comprehension. But He can reveal Himself to you if you let Him.

It seemed easier to allow myself to sink into my depression and feel alone with my thoughts. It seemed easier to distance myself from those closest to me. And for a period of time, it was okay to let myself feel angry and bitter. To let myself feel and acknowledge the weight of my emotions. To let myself weep and to mourn. To let myself grieve. To let myself yell. But it was also necessary to let myself acknowledge the shades of God.

Our journey taught me that, despite any trials and tribulations that we may encounter, God has fully equipped us. There is a time to weep. There is a time to mourn. There is a time to grieve. There is a time to be angry. But, we can overcome, we can conquer, we can endure, we can stand and rise. With God's grace, we can do more than just survive, we can thrive. Once we have wept and mourned, we can heal, we can laugh, we can rejoice, we can dance!

Acknowledgements

To my dear husband, thank you for always encouraging me and for being my rock and comfort despite your own grief. Come what may, I cannot thank God enough for joining us together as man and wife. I love you forever.

To my mom, you will always be my favorite nurse. Regardless of how "grown" I get, I am so thankful that I can always count on you to take care of me.

To my favorite Christie, although our journeys are different, they are yet so similar. I am eternally grateful for our friendship and sisterhood. You inspire me.

To my host of family and friends, I thank you for every visit, every text, every phone call, every prayer, and every word of encouragement. You all light up my life and I do not know what we would have done without you all.

www.ingramcontent.com/pod-product-compliance
Ingram Content Group UK Ltd.
Pitfield, Milton Keynes, MK11 3LW, UK
UKHW031333170125
4163UKWH00020B/324

9 798696 998626